Appalachia. According to popular mythology, it's a mountainous hold-over from colonial days, an all-white outlaw society mired in poverty and cliché jokes about family feuds. Throw in some stories about moonshine, add a few images of grimy coal miners and you're done. People who know better and try to preserve Appalachian history and culture are no match for developers greedy for more land and franchise locations. The process is irreversible, but the real story—hilariously funny, sometimes poignant, always surprising—can be told, savored and remembered.

Philip Hirsh was born in the era of the Great Depression, the son of wealthy parents who divided their time between suburban New York City and their horse farm in Appalachia. Servants were given the child-rearing responsibilities freeing his parents to ride, play golf and drink lots (and lots) of mint juleps. He ate with the servants and farmers, went to their homes, and became an observant fly-on-the wall. It was a life of stunning contrast that worked perfectly as long as nothing positive about servants or "locals" was ever spoken in front of his parents.

Fifty years later Hirsh went back to the Hollows looking for the families and descendants of those folks who gave him the stories. He wanted to be certain his recollections were accurate, and that people wouldn't mind if he published them. The result is more a romp than a read. The stories are vivid, often outrageously funny, but always true to the people and the mysterious, wonderful place called Appalachia.

Voices
from the
Hollow

Philip Reid Hirsh, Jr.

BUENA VISTA, VIRGINIA

To
Dorothy L. Cleek
1910–1937

3 5 7 9 10 8 6 4 2

Library of Congress Control Number: 2005938568
Voices from The Hollow
Philip Reid Hirsh, Jr.

p. cm.

1. Bath County, Virginia 1930–1960 2. Appalachia—United States
History—20th century. 3. The Homestead 1766–2005

I. Hirsh, Philip Reid, Jr. II. Title

ISBN-13: 978-0-9776841-0-6 (softcover : alk. paper)

ISBN-10: 0-9776841-0-5

Edited and Designed by Andrew Wolfe

Cover Design by Patricia Gibson

MARINER PUBLISHING
a division of
Mariner Media, Inc.
131 West 21st Street
Buena Vista, VA 24416-2716
http://www.marinermedia.com

This book is printed on acid free paper meeting the requirements of the American Standard for
Permanence of Paper for Printed Library Materials.
The Compass-Rose and Pen is a Trademark of Mariner Media, Inc.

Contents

Introduction   vii

Ashes in Ashes   1

Feelin' Juberous   23

The Cooper Field   73

Not You, Not Here   83

Taming of the Shrews   101

Heroes   107

Hold The Wheel, Boy   121

Paradise Temporarily Lost   143

Granny Cleek   159

Moonshine   191

Two Gorillas and a Bunch of Snakes   211

Lessons Learned   229

Skunk in the Lobby   237

Endings   249

Acknowledgements   259

End Notes   263

Introduction

In Appalachia it's called a "hollar," a place where geography and history got together to protect a people and their way of life from the outside world. The sun is in on it, too. In the deepest hollows it doesn't touch the bottom until midmorning, and within a couple of hours its warming rays start a rapid retreat. By late afternoon a smoky shadow covers the hollow and it starts to get dark.

It has always been a tough place to make a living; but adversity built the mountain character, and isolation preserved it well into the 20th century. But mountain barriers are no defense against the relentless pressure of a material society: the seductive power of television, instant oatmeal and salesmen hawking the glories of life in a double-wide trailer. Some say the flood of Great Society social workers finished the job by telling folks their way of life had to go, replacing it with dependence on the government they had resisted for so long. Maybe it was the collapse of King Coal, or the end of virgin timber forests.

It was all of that and more, but I'll leave the cultural questions to others. I want to tell you about folks I knew as a youngster, real people whose lives and stories are as powerful to me now as they were over a half a century ago. I began the project with several stories read on National Public Radio in Roanoke, Virginia, a station covering a large part of eastern Appalachia. The stories were well received and the station manager suggested I put them together as a book.

It seemed like a good idea, but it wasn't until the project was nearly complete that I understood just why. Like most of life's best insights this one hit me broadside when I least expected it. Old memories, no matter how vivid, are subject to distortion—that's obvious. So it was necessary to check my facts as best I could, given the huge gap in time between the late 1930's and now, and make sure that it was all right with the people involved to tell their stories.

I was working my way up a hollow on a narrow dirt road early one afternoon trying to find the home of a man who had worked for my grandmother when I was a kid. It had taken quite a while to locate him. He would have been well into his eighties, and I had no idea what shape his memory was in, or if he would even talk to me. Rumor had it his wife was feeling poorly, so I brought along some apple butter and home-made sausage.

The light was holding, but the embracing trees overhead made it more like a tunnel than a road. I finally found the house and was relieved to see the old man come out on the porch. I explained why I had come, and he invited me in. It was summer but the wood stove was cranked up and the front room was stiflingly hot.

His wife lay on the couch under several blankets. She didn't seem to notice us at all. It was an awful moment. Clearly, the woman was dying and I had blundered into the intimacy of their last moments together. I tried to leave but the old man would have none of it. He said he was glad to have the company and seemed happy to talk about the days, fifty years before, when he worked for "the old lady," as he called my grandmother.

We sat in the parlor and talked. I sweated and my head swam. It was clear he didn't want to leave the room and all the while we talked he kept his eyes on his wife. At the end of our talk, just as I was getting ready to go, he asked me a question.

"Philip, why do you want to tell 'bout us? Don't nobody care who we was or what we done."

Wham!

"No!" I said a little too loudly and without thinking about it. "You're important, your life is important. And I don't want it to be lost." We both looked at his wife, I choked, and he rescued me.

"Well, I reckon. I just never thought of it like that."

I left and made it out of the hollow without sliding off the road. To tell the truth I wasn't thinking about the road, I was feeling ashamed that I had been making the project about me. My title up to that point had been Tales from the Hollow. My tales, my stories. Suddenly it became clear. This isn't about me, I was just dumb-lucky enough to have been there to take it all in.

These are the voices of people who lived at the end of the old-time Appalachian culture. They are silent now, but they must not be forgotten.

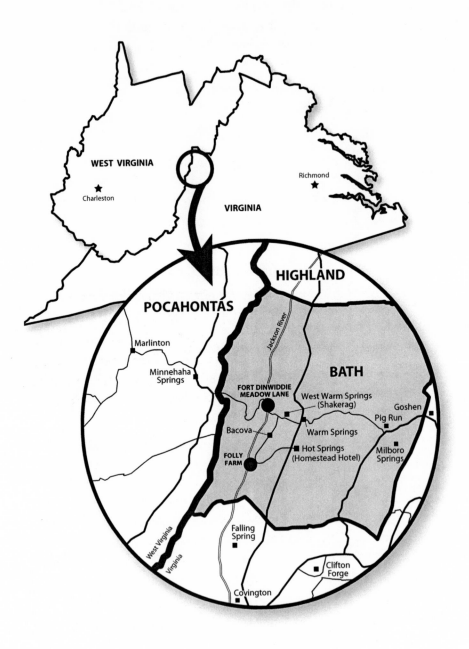

Chapter I

Ashes in Ashes

Grandfather's second funeral went wrong from the start.

I guess the first one went as planned, but I was thirteen, it was my first funeral, and the whole thing had me too scared to pay attention to details. No one close to me had died before. Death and funerals were abstractions, something that happened in other families, not mine. If there had been a misfire the first time around I wouldn't have known it.

Less than a week before, I had seen Grandfather in the hospital in New York City. He sat in an easy chair in pajamas and robe, newspapers and a smoldering cigar on the table next to him, flowers everywhere. His room was thirty stories above Morningside Drive with a downtown view of the West Side and Central Park. There were no IV poles, no pipes or wires sticking out of the wall, nothing to suggest impending death. It was as if we were visiting him at the Waldorf, not a hospital.

Father talked business, Mother fussed with the flowers, and I stared out the window. It was 1951 and there was no hospital TV, but outside a little snow was falling, and Christmas lights were visible as tiny color gashes far below. Grandfather's half-eaten dinner sat on a gleaming silver tray on a table by the door waiting for a waiter to pick it up. Father explained that Grandfather found hospital food offensive, so he had lunch and dinner brought to him from his favorite restaurant, *Chambord*, on 3rd Avenue.

"If I have to die, at least it won't be from the food," he told my father. Knowing how he felt about food, I don't doubt the story.

Then suddenly he was dead, and I was about to attend his funeral. But first there was an emergency trip to DePinna's to be fitted for my funeral suit, a dark and scratchy thing I subsequently wore with dread, and was happy to outgrow. Aside from a few weddings, the interior of a church was an unfamiliar place to me. It puzzled me at the time that my equally non-church-going grandfather was being given a send-off at St. Luke's Episcopal Church.

The family entered the church through the back door. A man dressed in the blackest suit I had ever seen led us down a long hallway to some sort of dressing room behind and to one side of the altar. It was mid-December, the room was cold as ice, and there was no place to sit. I tried desperately to become invisible, but being the only child in that cramped space made the adults want to ask me over and over if I was all right. I was so choked I could only bob my head, stare at my feet, and hope they would leave me alone.

Suddenly the minister loomed in the doorway dressed in an enormous ornate robe covered by what looked like a tablecloth. He wore an unctuous smile, spoke in a whisper, and shook hands all around. Finally, he got to me. I bravely put out my hand, but he ignored it; instead, he grabbed my trembling shoulders and spun me around to face the others.

"It's always hardest on the young," he said in a louder voice. Everyone stared at me. I was the only one in the place under thirty so there was no mistaking about whom he was speaking. Suddenly there was no air left in the room.

Standing in the hallway were four choirboys wearing lace ponchos, carrying candles and looking bored. They were totally deadpan as if this was something they did every day. Worse, one was a classmate. Crying in front of a friend! Dear God! How bad can this get? Maybe they'll throw in a penicillin shot. Never before had I felt so conspicuous and downright miserable.

The minister said a prayer and we marched into the front of the church. The house was packed to its oak rafters, and Grandfather's coffin was positioned in front of the altar, barely visible under a blanket of flowers. I wasn't prepared for the coffin, and even though it was closed, it finished off what little control I had left.

We filed into the front pews and I spent the next hour staring at the closed mahogany box a scant five feet in front of me, trying to cry as quietly as possible. Like someone trying not to think about a dancing bear, I couldn't stop using my X-ray vision to see inside the box. It actually helped ease the misery to focus on the box and not on the prayers and throbbing church organ.

I had never seen a dead person, much less one I knew. Was he still in his pajamas? Did he smell funny? Was his mouth open or closed? Was he *really* dead or did they box him up prematurely? Maybe he was trying to get out, but the flowers were too heavy for him in his weakened state. There had been no funeral home event, no open casket, so my disobedient imagination kept prying open the box to see what Grandfather looked like in death.

Finally it was over, and we all went to our house for what looked to me like a huge party, complete with bartender and two maids passing watercress sandwiches with the crusts cut off, and little disks of something red with fish eggs on top. There was no trip to the graveyard, and no prayers from the minister who was there dressed in regular clothes. He was also having a drink. Maybe two.

Before I disappeared to my room, I asked my mother what had become of Grandfather? Was he left in the church to be dealt with later? Or did we skip the graveyard to get directly to the party? I was told he would be cremated, something I did not fully understand, but I certainly wasn't about to ask any more questions. It came with a scary enough visual as it was.

"We'll bury his ashes on the farm after Christmas, dear. I'm sorry, but you'll have to miss a few days of school."

Things were finally starting to look up. I was going to miss school without having my appendix taken out, *and* I was going on the overnight sleeper train to the farm in Virginia, my favorite place in the entire world. All I had to do was make it through one more funeral. And this time around there was no church involved, it was all outside. The death thing was getting easier to handle.

My grandparents owned two large farms, Meadow Lane and Fort Dinwiddie, in Warm Springs, Virginia, where they bred horses and raised sheep. Grandfather had grown up in Richmond in the late nineteenth century. When he was a kid in the 1880's, his parents often traveled to the mountains on the western edge of the state "to take the waters" in the spas of Bath County.

Such a trip was a major undertaking in its day. First, there was the train from Richmond to Goshen, itself a well-known spa, where the family spent the night. In the morning they boarded a stagecoach for the thirty-mile trip to Warm Springs, the highlight of which was the ride up, over and down the extremely steep Warm Springs Mountain.

At the top of the mountain, the stage stopped at a tollgate and was prepared for the hair-raising run through a series of switchbacks to the bottom of the mountain. To keep the stagecoach from running away down the mountain, one of the back wheels was chained in place, and a second brakeman was added. He braced his feet on the dash and hauled back on the brake handle with all his strength. By the time they reached the bottom, the leather brakes were burned to the shaft, and the brakeman was exhausted.

People gathered on the porch of the Warm Springs Hotel to watch the stage through gaps in the trees and listen to the sounds of the brakes, dragging wheel, horses—and (as one contemporary observer put it) the screams of the passengers "dithering from fright." Grandfather said that of all his childhood memories, the stagecoach ride down Warm Springs Mountain was his absolute favorite. He said that on one of those rides he promised himself that when he grew up he would buy property near Warm Springs.

And he did, so it was no surprise to anyone that he wanted to be buried there.

Bath County borders West Virginia about midway down the western edge of Virginia. It's a mountainous place, full of springs and long empty hollows, small farms. Like much of Appalachia, it is isolated from the outside world by topography, a short growing season and an absence of any industry. Warm Springs is the county seat, and in 1952 had a population of about three hundred. Even today, there isn't a single traffic light in the entire county.[1]

Every spot in the road is named after its spring: Hot Springs, Warm Springs, Healing Springs, Cedar Springs, Falling Springs, etc. The county's only major business, the Homestead Hotel, claims its origin in the area's warm springs, a history that began in the 1760's during "troublous times" when Indians were still a major threat on the western edge of Colonial Virginia. Everything to the west was Indian territory. By a 1763 order, George III proclaimed it illegal to settle west of the fall line—territory beyond the headwaters of any river flowing east to the Atlantic. So Bath County was as far as a settler could legally go.

The line was guarded by a thin chain of forts strung along the frontier, each exactly one half-day ride from the other. The theory was if you got caught by Indians in between forts, you were always able to race to one fort or the other in daylight. Fort Dinwiddie was just west of Warm Springs on the Jackson River below the headwaters of the James River. According to the highway historical marker, it was built in 1755 and visited in that year by Lieutenant George Washington. Every family should have its own George Washington-slept-here story.

Grandfather bought the fort and the surrounding five thousand acres piece by piece starting around WWI. It was paradise for a kid. I could disappear for chunks of unsupervised time at the barns, go fishing in the river, or (if my grandmother didn't catch me) hang out with the grooms, field hands and house servants who made the whole operation work. But getting there was best of all. It meant taking the Cincinnati-bound C&O railroad overnight from our home in New Jersey to Hot Springs.

The great diesel always rumbled into Newark's Penn Station at exactly 7:05 p.m., and the engineer never failed to wave. We went immediately to the dining car for dinner. To me, there was no restaurant in the world to compare with the C&O dining car. I was allowed a rare strip steak and a Coke—the perfect meal. Soft drinks were banned in our house, but for some reason the rule was relaxed on the train. Bliss.

After dinner we went to our cabins. Mine was always made up early so I could immediately turn out the lights, lie on the bed, listen to the sounds of the train, and watch the night world slide by. In the stations, people on the platform couldn't see into the blackened room, and I became The Shadow spying on unknowing passengers only inches away. I fought sleep, but the soporific rhythm of the rails usually knocked me out before Washington.

About 5:00 AM the Hot Springs car was separated from the train and sat silently for an hour on a siding in Clifton Forge. That was my signal to get up and wait for the great steam engine to bring a baggage car, connect up, and take us the last twenty-five miles up the spur line to Hot Springs for a never-fail arrival at 8:00 AM. Most of the passengers were headed for the Homestead Hotel and, like my parents, didn't get up until the last minute. After all, Hot Springs was the end of the line so there was no hurry to get off.

I couldn't understand why anyone would want to miss the steam engine or the slow ride up through the valley. But I was often the only one up, and the conductor let me ride in the baggage car, its great door wide open with only a safety rope to hang on to. Mailbags were plucked from poles as the train lazed along. The baggage men usually had a bucket of bones to throw in great flying arcs to dogs who raced across meadows eager to get their morning treat.

We had spent that Christmas in St. Croix, and New Year's duck hunting in Maryland. By mid-January my grief had subsided and I was ready for the second funeral. Should be easy, I thought: a quick trip up the hill for the burial of the ashes, and while the family has its cocktail party I'll slip over to the new manager's house for some real food, and maybe go squirrel hunting with my new buddy, Glenn, the manager's son.

I should have guessed it wouldn't go as planned. It turned out to be almost as bad as Grandfather's third funeral.

But it started well: the ride down on the C&O was perfect. True to form, my parents, three uncles and their wives, and several of Grandfather's close friends, all stayed in their beds until the train was close to Hot Springs. I was up and in the baggage car as we pulled out of Clifton Forge.

I had never ridden up the valley in winter, and the fact the open door made the baggage car freezing cold only added to the adventure. The dogs' bones had frozen together and when the baggage man stomped them apart they flew in every direction. I almost fell out the door trying to snag them, but one of the men grabbed me and said I'd never make a baggage man if I couldn't stay on my feet. We all thought that was terribly funny. I remember that moment with total clarity. Had anything vaguely similar happened at home I would have been blasted by Father for my carelessness. Not here. We were three guys standing in the open door of the swaying baggage car throwing bones and sharing a laugh.

And my parents were sound asleep.

When we arrived at the farm, the servants, grooms and the rest of the employees were all lined up on the front porch, somber and genuinely sad. One of the maids, Alice, cried and gave me a hug. I felt badly that my mood didn't match hers. But thinking about it, she had more to grieve than I; after all, my generally good-natured grandfather was gone, and now they were all under my grandmother's hammer. If ever there were a scary, demanding, self-focused person, it was my grandmother. Everyone was terrified of her, especially me. There were no other grandchildren until I was almost 10, no little buffers to share the heat. Even her four sons seemed intimidated, and while they complained about her when she wasn't around, they rarely stood up to her.

"Children should be seen and not heard" was one of her favorite sayings. I did my best to avoid both.

The only one who seemed immune to her was Grandfather. I think it suited his image to be seen as the funny, reasonable, generous alternative to "The Madam," as she was known behind her back. He was definitely the good cop. The employees all knew Grandfather well, enjoyed his jocular nature and seemed relaxed around him.

With my grandfather,
Allan Mortimer Hirsh, 1878-1951.
In personality, the opposite of the
Madam.

It was a different story with Grandmother. Except for the gardener and household servants, Grandmother rarely spoke to the other workers. Dottie Cutlip, the daughter of one of Grandfather's farm managers, grew up within a half-mile of the main house, yet she doesn't recall ever speaking to my grandmother, much less being introduced to her. Still, she and her brother and sisters were frightened to death of her. The Madam's invisibility and trio of enormous Great Danes only added to her scary reputation. Dottie and her siblings always took the long way around her house on the way to and from the school bus, terrified the Danes would run them down.

Grandmother was totally indifferent to what anyone working on the farm might think of her—or anything else, for that matter. She lavished affection on her dogs, but not on people. When she returned from a trip she always greeted each dog before any of her four children. Because her Danes were show dogs, they were treated like royalty, and when a big show was afoot nothing else (short of a house fire) could get her attention.

The Madam's three Great Danes, more precious than any child.
Taken in the late 1930's.

The dogs won regularly. Perhaps it would be more accurate to say she won regularly, and she didn't suffer competition gracefully. In the early 1920's a Dane from Hawaii was winning every show on the west coast, and threatening to come east to challenge the Madam's iron grip on the Best in Show trophy. She took a train to California, met the owner and offered to buy the dog. The price was $3000, take it or leave it. She didn't bat an eye, bought the dog, returned home and made him a house pet. He never set paw in the ring again.

Personality-wise, Grandfather was a polar opposite. He cultured the *bonhomme* image of a cheerful, easy-going, approachable boss. He had a stern side, and I was wary of it, but even when he was cross it had a benign feel. The Madam lived in a state of perpetual annoyance, her hair-trigger anger instant and scorching. Grandfather, on the other hand, was rarely upset, and when he was, he came across more like an impatient teacher than an inflamed snapping turtle. He also had a passive-aggressive way of undermining the Madam, something that gave all of us—family members and servants alike—immense voyeuristic satisfaction.

"Let's go fishing!" he would say to the house staff when Grandmother was off the farm. We all piled in an old Plymouth, rods sticking out of every window, me on someone's lap, and bounced down the dirt road to the river. Grandmother would return to an empty house, explode, and head for the bell.

There were two bells at their house. One was a mini Liberty Bell mounted on a pole, a stout rope hanging nearly to the ground. That was the fire bell. The other was a Bermuda carriage bell rung by stamping a foot plunger. It was mounted in a wooden frame on the front porch. It was high pitched, loud, and if the breeze was right, it could be heard all the way to the fishing hole. When we heard it, we packed up and returned, laughing playfully knowing Grandfather would deal with the Madam.

He was the only one who could shut her up. He had some sort of internal fed-up meter, and when she went over the invisible line, he would stamp his foot or slam his fist on the table and say: "Oh, Ellen, shut up!" And she did, at least for a few minutes.

Breakfast the morning of the funeral was very weird. The servants' grief had retriggered some of my own sadness, but the rest of the family and friends were all in fine spirits. They didn't even seem to notice that Grandfather's place was set, water was poured in his glass, and with each course his plates were changed as if he were sitting in the empty chair.

I wanted to scream! Didn't anyone think this was a little bizarre? Apparently not, because no one said a thing about it. And it wasn't one of those things you see but pretend you don't. No, sir, they saw it, but somehow it seemed normal to them.

After breakfast, a man from the C&O showed up to go over the funeral plan. I had heard it said that a train was to be involved, but foolishly I thought that referred to the fact we were all arriving by train, including Grandfather, whose ashes made the trip in a picnic hamper.

Wrong. There was a grander and far more convoluted plan. At noon the next day we were to drive to Covington—an awful thirty-mile ride on a curvy mountain road made worse by the nauseating stench of the paper mill in Covington. I had been sick many times on that road.

We were supposed to be picked up in Covington by the Hot Springs train after it returned to Clifton Forge and was turned around in the great roundhouse. A passenger car was added and the baggage car dropped. We were to be the only passengers, and with no baggage car, that meant no place for me to hide.

A minister was going to stand on the rear platform, say prayers, and sprinkle little whiffs of Grandfather into the valley air as we crept back up to Hot Springs. Then we were to go out to the farm, up to the top of Fort Dinwiddie hill, and finally the urn and presumably a few remaining crumbs were to be buried by a huge river rock hauled up the hill to the newly fenced in Final Resting Place. Exactly where the urn wound up in the FRP was to become the pivot in Grandfather's third, and in some ways, most bizarre funeral.

After the C&O man left and I could safely disappear, I went to the manager's house. Frank Williams had recently been hired to begin converting the farm from horses to cattle. Grandmother was in a twit about the livestock idea, "common" she called it. She took her horses and Shropshire sheep and moved them to her own farm about five miles away.

Over the years the Williams family became as important to me as my own family. And Frank Williams was—and remains—a true hero to me. When Frank heard me describe the funeral plan he laughed and asked, "How in the world do they plan to get to the top of the hill?" It was January, but the weather was moderating, the ground was thawing, and the orchard grass was wet, and very slick. As it turned out they should have consulted Frank.

The next morning we drove to Covington. I begged for a front seat to minimize the nausea factor, but the request was denied. How about an open window? Too cold. I knew I would be in a heap of trouble if I puked on my funeral suit so I fought hard and managed to hold down my breakfast.

We got to the station fifteen minutes early. Father, typically irritable and anxious, paced up and down the platform checking his watch every twenty seconds. We huddled on wooden benches on the platform. The station was closed so we couldn't wait inside. Worse, there was no bathroom.

"Where the hell are Malcolm and that goddamned minister? And whose bright idea was it to have Malcolm drive him down here?" Father grumbled to no one in particular. Mother told him to calm down, but I sensed there was trouble afoot. Even I knew that

Uncle Malcolm loved a wee drink in the morning. When we heard the great steam whistle in the distance and felt the ground begin to tremble, and there was still no sign of Malcolm, the minister, or the ashes, I knew trouble had gone from brewing to a full boil.

The train rumbled into the station and we climbed aboard. Father and the stationmaster got into a heated argument. The train had to leave in that instant, it was an unscheduled train and absolutely could not sit on the main line another minute. At the very least it would have to go up the Hot Springs spur, stop and wait. And that meant a long walk up the tracks for Malcolm and the preacher.

Father lost the argument, and the train started to inch forward just as Malcolm's car pulled into the parking lot. As they got out it was suddenly clear what had caused the delay. They were both crocked. Father was screaming at them to hurry, but they were laughing and in no shape to run. The minister had his arms around what looked like a hefty brass flowerpot, but somehow they managed to struggle on board literally as the train left the station.

Father was livid, the guests were obviously uncomfortable, Malcolm's wife was in tears, and I was still fighting with my breakfast. Father's two other brothers got him calmed down, the preacher seemed to get a grip, and as the train gathered speed, we all moved toward the rear platform. There wasn't much room out there, but somehow we squeezed together and Funeral Number Two was under way.

The minister unscrewed the top of the urn, held it over his head, and with eyes closed, began a prayer. At that exact moment the train lurched, and the urn flew out of the preacher's fingers up into the air, and fell upside down dead square in the center of the rail bed. By the time the conductor signaled the engineer and he got the train stopped, the urn was just a tiny brass speck in the distance.

Father, never one to wait, jumped off and started running back toward the urn. The engineer reversed the train and we rolled back, quickly passing Father. The train stopped about 50 yards from the urn and the men climbed down and formed a circle around the dented vessel. The ashes—a huge volume, it seemed to me—were now mixed with the gravel, dirt and toilet paper between the tracks.

Father arrived puffing like a seal, the minister kept apologizing, and Grandmother was yelling something from the back of the train. We all got down on our knees and tried to get Grandfather back in the urn a few crumbs at a time. Only a fraction of the ashes were recovered, not nearly enough for the symbolic spreading and burial, so some dirt was scraped up and added to the urn.

Everyone climbed back on board and we lumbered away, leaving the rest of Grandfather between the tracks clinging to oil-soaked gravel and those melting wads of toilet paper.

Inside the passenger car people sat in little groups, their enthusiasm for prayers and ash spreading completely dashed. We rode in silence the rest of the way to Hot Springs. At least my nausea was gone.

From Hot Springs, we drove to the farm and gathered at the base of Dinwiddie hill. The temperature was well above freezing, the grass was wet, and the ground—at least the surface—had begun to thaw. There was gathering doubt about the ability of the cars to get up the hill, so Father and his brothers went up for a test run.

They did fine on the lower part of the hill, but as the incline grew steeper they slowed, and about three-quarters of the way up they stopped completely. Then, ever so slowly, the car started to come back down the hill—backwards. At first it looked like a controlled retreat, but as they gathered speed, it was clear they were in trouble. The rear end veered slightly to one side, the car turned and continued to slide down sideways. It finally stopped at the foot of the hill about ten yards from where they started.

After a quick conference, they sent for the farm jeep, a WWII-vintage Willys. It was getting late, so it was decided that only Grandmother, her four sons and their wives, and the now sober and contrite minister would mount the hill. They were ferried up in shifts while the rest of us waited below. But we didn't have to wait long: they were back and ready for a drink in under fifteen minutes.

So I missed the end of the funeral, which in some ways was too bad, because if I had been there I might have noticed exactly where in relation to the huge rock the urn was actually buried. Twenty-five years later that could have saved a lot of trouble.

My grandmother persisted into her ninety-seventh year before dying in her sleep at home. In her entire life she had never been in a hospital, and aside from self-administered chloroform for childbirth, she is only known to have taken medicine once. At eighty-nine she sprained her ankle, and the doctor advised an aspirin which she angrily refused. He pushed her to accept a half of a tablet, and she relented. He should have left well enough alone: about an hour later she said she felt dizzy from the doctor's "dope," as she called it. She fired him and never spoke to him again.

She also refused to be buried on the hill with Grandfather. Over the years the plot had fallen into disrepair. The split rail fence was down, and the rock, big as it was, disappeared in a huge tangle of multiflora roses and poison ivy. Periodically, someone would take a stab at cleaning out the spot, but when the Madam died it was a hopeless tangle of roots, vines and undergrowth.

In spite of her years, her death was unexpected, and suddenly the question of what to do with Grandfather arose. It seemed awkward to bury Grandmother in the Warm Springs cemetery and leave her husband to be forgotten on the hill, so they decided to dig him up and bury their ashes together, the urns side-by-side in a special black box provided by the funeral director. Seems this sort of arrangement wasn't all that unusual.

And there was plenty of time, two days until the funeral.

The first day was spent getting equipment up the hill, clearing the vegetation to expose the rock and the ground around it. Then came the question of exactly where to dig for the urn. Of the original ten who saw the burial in the fading light of that chaotic Saturday in 1952, death and divorce had reduced the number to three: Father, his older brother Allan, and youngest brother Malcolm.

In the morning the day before the funeral, the digging began. But the roots of the just-cleared trees and bushes made it very tough going. By mid afternoon there were dozens of shallow holes, but no sign of the urn. The anxiety level skyrocketed.

Father finally broke and went off to fetch the backhoe, his favorite farm tool, and one he handled with considerable skill. The yellow beast finally made it up the hill and the *real* digging began. First a minimal scoop to pull up some of the roots; that went off to one side. Then a bigger scoop. Then another, and another. Finally the giant rock was pushed away and its underside excavated.

Nothing. Anxiety had now turned to panic. A metal detector was brought in. And at last, just about dark, the elusive vessel was unearthed. Where? In the very first small scoop that had been dumped aside. The urn was barely under the surface, far too obvious to notice. If you want to hide something, put it out in the open where everyone can see it.

We came down the hill tired and relieved, foolishly thinking the problem was solved.

The Madam's funeral was scheduled for eleven the next day at St. Luke's in Hot Springs (same saint, different church). At eight the next morning Grandfather's battered, near-empty urn was delivered to the funeral home. But to everyone's horror, the urn was too big to allow the box to close. The only box in the place that would hold both together was a child's coffin. But it was bright white and covered with roses and little angels. The funeral was now only hours away, so there was no time to find an alternative.

Uncle Malcolm, perhaps to redeem himself for his role in the train incident, stepped up to save the day. To understand just *how* he did it requires a brief digression into the convoluted and unpredictable life of Malcolm McCallum Hirsh.

Malcolm was the youngest of the three surviving boys (the next in line, Jack, was killed in a car crash in 1957), and while a wonderfully funny, outgoing man, his performance in school and business was a bit uneven, though not without a few high spots.

According to family lore, he was tossed out of the Harvey School, a pre-prep boarding school in Katonah, New York. The reason? Most likely grades and/or general screwing around, but according to the family line, he was running a still in his closet, it exploded and ripped a wall out of the dorm. All of this at the age of 12? I doubt it.

He did finish Lawrenceville (high point), went to Washington and Lee College in the fall of 1941 (high point), but struggled with grades and withdrew five months later (low point). He joined the Army Air Corps, and served two-plus years (high point with an asterisk; more on that later). According to family lore, his father got him into Yale but supposedly he left within a month. Actually, he lasted almost six months, but either way, that was the end of his college career (low point).

He did not return to Washington and Lee, though he claimed the class of 1945 as his own. That was not an uncommon practice for students in WWII whose studies were interrupted by the war. In 1995, at the 50th reunion of the class of 1945, he received an honorary degree (very high point).

One bit of history about Malcolm's educational career is not in dispute. In 1945, when it was clear Malcolm was not going to continue a college career, his parents decided to endow a scholarship at W&L "in honor of their son, an alumnus" for a "deserving student from Bath County." While they were alive, they of course reserved the right to "nominate" that deserving student.

Malcolm's sons have letters from grateful Bath County students helped by the fund. The *Bath County* (VA) *Scholarship* still exists.

Malcolm's two older brothers never missed a chance to say something negative about him, but none of it seemed to bother him at all. He bumped along in his own wacky way armed with plenty of money, an impulsive investment style, and a fabulous sense of humor. At one time he had owned a foundry, an Arizona desert resort, part of a clothing chain, and a hay business. But by far his most peculiar purchase was the town of Bacova, near Warm Springs (BAth COunty VA), two miles from Meadow Lane and Fort Dinwiddie.

Originally a company town for the Tidewater Hardwood Company, it was built in 1920, and supported two to three hundred people. Over 60 miles of narrow gauge railroad laced the valley bringing in enormous loads of virgin timber, mostly white oak. Two behemoth steam engines drove band saws producing over 100,000 feet of lumber every day. Workers were paid in company script good for everything from medical care from the company doctor to the collection plate at Bacova Chapel, the company's non-denominational church. The town sported a baseball team, a school, and a volunteer fire department.

The town persisted after the lumber company went out of business in the early part of the Great Depression. The price of lumber had fallen dramatically with the crash of 1929, and the company's efficient cutting, hauling and processing systems had all but stripped the area forests making it more costly to haul in smaller, more inaccessible trees. A salvage company ripped up the railroad track, scrapped the saws, five railroad engines and 200 railroad cars. Ironically, the metal was sold to Japan just before WWII. [2]

Two local men bought the town from Tidewater in the 1940's and rented the houses to folks who worked at the Homestead or on its many dairy and grain farms. When Malcolm bought it in August, 1959, Bacova had fallen on hard times. Most of the houses were in terrible shape, a few had fallen down, the Homestead was going out of the farming business, and there weren't many renters left. When Malcolm got it, there were 43 houses, along with the church, post office/general store, and the two-story commissary building. The road through was still dirt, and the rent on the houses was under ten dollars a month. Buying it looked to everyone like a fool's game.

Virgin white oak logs at the Tidewater Hardwood mill in Bacova, mid-1920's. (Photo courtesy of the Bath County Historical Society).

But Malcolm was undaunted. He bought a vintage fire truck, and after a few drinks he would put on his fireman's hat, crank up the hand-turned siren, and drive around his town. Asked on **What's My Line?** exactly why he bought the place, he replied it was because he always wanted to be a town fire chief. No one guessed him ("Will The *Real* Malcolm Hirsh Please Stand Up!") and he collected $100 after his moment of fame on national television.

Bacova resident Whit Bogan demonstrates the size of a stack of lumber,
just a fraction of a single day's output, 1928.
(Photo courtesy of Mary Bogan Broce).

Over time, he invested heavily in the town, and fixed up every house, the church and the commissary. He raised the rents only fractionally, and within five years the place was wide-awake and completely refurbished. He then started selling the houses to renters for nominal amounts. He sank a lot of money into the place, the people there loved him for it, and today Bacova is a charming and vibrant little village. A new town playground has recently been named in honor of Malcolm, another high point, and well deserved.

But the commissary posed a problem. It was a substantial two-story building, about 100 feet long, abandoned for many years, yet still in good condition. All it needed was a coat of paint and a good business. Somewhere along the line Malcolm met a silk screen artist who did cutesy animal and bird pictures, and together they cooked up the idea of embedding wildlife pictures in a sheet of fiberglass, then wrapping it around a mailbox. The idea worked, and suddenly they were cranking out boxes by the hundred in the old Tidewater commissary.

Before a mailbox got its fiberglass armor it had to be painted dull black. This was done with a conveyor belt and an automated paint sprayer system. Moving slow-motion, each box was first spray painted, then sent through a hot air wind tunnel. Start to dry finish, the process took about an hour.

Back at the funeral home, about two hours before the Madam's funeral, the two urns were locked in the child's coffin padded with towels from the dry goods store so they wouldn't rattle around when moved (hearing sounds coming from a locked coffin is disconcerting). The coffin was then taken to Bacova and put on the conveyor belt. It didn't make it in time for the church service, but when we arrived at the graveyard the jet-black box was already in the open hole. Prayers were said, the hole was closed, and it was finally over. With a little luck there won't be a fourth funeral for Grandfather.

Chapter II

Feelin' Juberous

I was pushing three in the summer of 1941. Most of my memories from that time are little more than picture fragments, but some are clear Technicolor images as strong as last night's dream. Because my life was so thoroughly regimented, its routine repeated each day shifting only to accommodate a change in place or characters, that entire summer comes back as a series of images like a jerky film clip. I certainly couldn't have identified the year from the memories alone, but when added to family photos, stories and most importantly, long talks years later with many of the key players, I can put these early pictures in an accurate perspective.

This is an important point, not simply to keep the narrative true to events, but because of the life-long impact the first summers in Appalachia had on my thinking. It was the start of a cumulative process that ultimately saved me from becoming another vector in the family dysfunction, a kind of pathology based on elitism, intense prejudice, and an over-inflated sense of our own importance. The pain of differentiating from the family's enshrined ideology was intense, especially for my father who saw my movement away from cherished assumptions as disloyalty and rebellion. My modest successes in school and choice of a career in medicine instead of engineering made him uncomfortable, even resentful—though he didn't say so out loud.

I wasn't the only one who felt the censoring weight of Father's sensitivity to challenge. Mother's family had an entirely different, more egalitarian set of ideals, but they were so thoroughly ridiculed she rarely spoke of them at home. Her mother's Presbyterian ancestors had been missionaries in India. Her great aunt, Ida Scudder, was in the first class to graduate women from Cornell Medical School. After Cornell she joined her family in India, and founded a woman's medical college. I have a 1973 Ripley's *Believe It or Not!* newspaper clipping about Ida Scudder. It says she was "so popular in India that letters from America reached her in a land of 350,000,000 people addressed to 'Dr. Ida, India.'"

She may have been popular in India, but not in my father's house. He regarded her as a religious eccentric, and saw Mother's heavy hand in my decision to go to medical school. He tended to see these matters in competitive terms, and took points off for disloyalty.

I couldn't possibly have shaped the idea and said it back then, but from the start I was growing up in two worlds, one split between place, the other between people. On a geographic level, I was living an urban life centered in northern New Jersey and New York City, and a less frequent life on the edge of eastern Appalachia. It was the stark contrast between the two, particularly between my family and the people in the mountains of Virginia, which shaped the direction of my life.

The *dramatis personae* in New Jersey were a predictable crowd. On the surface, they all seemed to be rowing more-or-less in comfortable unison with no particular concern over who might be in the lead at any given moment. But when no one was looking, they would sneak in an extra stroke or two trying to gain a little distance on the others. The kids all went to the same schools, everyone over thirteen owned a tuxedo, and dancing anything beyond a waltz or fox trot was considered pretty edgy. Even the servants fit into the scheme. They all knew each other, had Sunday off, and worried when someone in the system was sick.

The story in western Virginia was completely different. My relatives assumed that, like trees falling silently in an empty forest, if they weren't around all was quiet. They would have scoffed at the idea there was a vibrant, cohesive culture there with its own language, music and traditions. Even my grandfather, who knew the area well, would have rejected the culture idea. He often said the place had a certain "character," a kind of bucolic charm born of being "backward," ignorant of the outside world. A great area to recruit naïve and faithful workers, maybe, but a place with history and values that might rival his own? Nonsense!

Even more consequential than location was the two-tiered way I was being raised. Not unlike many well-to-do families, we had servants to do virtually all the heavy lifting and day-to-day running of the household. They cooked, served the meals, cleaned, drove us around, gardened, and most importantly: took care of the children. Since at that point I was my parent's only child—and for my first decade the family's only grandchild—it meant that no matter whose house we were in, I was automatically in the care of people I had grown to know well.

They were a durable and very loyal group of people. Most worked for us for decades. One woman, Alice Fortune, came to work for my grandmother just after WWI when she was about twenty. She stayed with the family until Grandmother died in 1977. Many of the conversations I had with her, especially after Grandmother died, were more open and fruitful than any I ever had with either my mother or father. Alice parted with family secrets with the greatest reluctance, but over time I learned more from her about what went on behind the scenes than I could from anyone else. Even so, there were many facts and recollections she held onto. I had to respect her boundaries even though I often felt tantalizingly close to some historical family morsel, a tidbit that would flesh out some suspicion or even open up new, unsuspected areas of interest.

But Alice took those remnants to the grave. When she died at the age of 98, I felt the loss of a friend, confidant, and alter parent. Her reward for sixty years of service, by the way, was a used VW Beetle, and a paltry $10,000 in cash.

The job of raising me, literally from the moment I came home from the hospital, fell to live-in "nurse maids" and servants, women who wore white or gray uniforms, white stockings and functional shoes. My parents orchestrated and monitored the process, but their emotional involvement was tangential. They certainly loved me and were glad to have me around, but the rules of child rearing dictated the work part be delegated, thus freeing the parents to enjoy and nurture their offspring free of the inconvenience of dirty diapers and early morning feedings.

It never occurred to them that the diaper-feeding-bathing time had anything to do with bonding, affection and the molding of personality. It should have been no mystery why I was from the start so close to the maids who cooed me through my bath, and later took me on long chatty walks, or sang sweet and funny ditties my tone-deaf parents couldn't even hum.

When Mother read to me it was usually a bedtime story about some idiot child jumping over an open flame, or a night-terror tale about an enormous creature chasing a small child around the house in hopes of eating him. Then she capped it off with the nightly prayer including the comforting lines:

If I should die before I wake,

I pray the Lord my soul to take.

On the front porch at Meadow Lane Farm, Christmas, 1935. The Madam's note on the back of this picture simply says: "Our employees, Christmas '35." Alice Fortune is on the right, back row.

Swell. If Fe Fi Fo Fum didn't eat you, this Lord character might snatch you when you're asleep. And my mother wondered why I always stayed clear of religion!

Another stumper for them was my caution around Father. To his friends he was a fun-loving storyteller, always ready with a good joke and another Scotch. To me he was touchy, stern, critical, and had an incendiary temper. He was also unpredictable. I never quite knew when he would lash out; often, he let major infractions slip by but exploded over something seemingly trivial. It was that element of surprise and the frightening energy behind it that made me super-vigilant, always trying to anticipate and avoid anything that might make him erupt. Mother, too, seemed cowed by his anger, though she clearly had her own passive-aggressive ways of dealing with him. But this was never discussed, not even after they divorced when I was in my mid-twenties.

Late in his life—looking back—Father said his favorite thing to do was fire people. Discipline was his game, something he approached with considerable relish. Any infraction was punishable with a tongue lashing, and it didn't take much to earn a nasty spanking. He also thought it character building to spank a child on his birthday, one swat for each year plus "one to grow on." That hateful ritual persisted until I was twelve.

By contrast no maid ever laid a hand on me. If I did something wrong, all it took to correct me was a hint that, at least momentarily, I had lost their affection. And as quickly as I corrected myself, the affection returned. As far as stories went, they preferred telling or singing to reading.

I usually saw my parents early in the morning then again in the evening. Father worked in his father's engineering firm; Mother volunteered at the Red Cross, went to Junior League meetings and played endless games of golf and bridge. After someone bathed and dressed me, Mother reviewed the results. Once properly polished, I could be seen briefly by friends or family, declared a precious little darling, and sent off with the maid. I was extraordinarily polite and diffident around my parents, something their friends often noted; indeed, their parenting skills were widely acclaimed.

There were other family illusions. The chief family illusionist was my grandfather, "Pop" Hirsh. As a kid I often heard him described as a gourmet chef. While he loved good food, belonged to the *Club 21* luncheon group and had an enormous wine cellar, I never saw him chop an onion or stir a pot. But he was a consummate showman with a perfect sense of timing and the resources to stage any imaginable drama.

Take cooking duck, for example. A gleaming silver duck press stood atop the sideboard in my grandparents' dining room. It looked like a miniature cider press held up by a burley lion's

The Madam in formal sidesaddle pose, early 1920's.

clawed feet, its barrel deeply engraved with ornate hunting scenes. Wild ducks were plentiful in those days, and hunting them was a popular family sport. After a shoot, the butler plucked and gutted the birds, and the cook roasted them and put all the ingredients for the sauce in little dishes. The breast and legs were removed, the carcass was placed in the press and, with great fanfare, Grandfather turned the silver wheel. Everyone oo'd and ahh'd as the juices flowed. He stirred the prepared ingredients in a chafing dish, then served up the reserved meat and sauce with a caution to be careful not to break a tooth on a piece of shot.

There was wide agreement that no one cooked a better duck than Pop Hirsh.

I saw the performance many times as a kid and it always buffaloed me how he got so much mileage out of twisting a silver wheel. I was taking it literally, of course, too young to grasp the metaphor or understand the power of theater.

When summer arrived we all went to the farm in Virginia. Father and Grandfather went back and forth to New Jersey every other week or so, my three unmarried uncles came and went, but my mother and grandmother stayed the entire time. Later in the summer my parents took a vacation from their vacation, and left me for a few weeks while they went to Europe.

Summer to the family was one long romp, time off to play more games of golf, ride horses, socialize and do a lot of drinking. They brought their urban life to the country, and while their costumes were slightly less formal, they didn't change their thinking or behavior one bit. They were just as cranky and competitive with each other five miles up a dirt road in Appalachia as they were in Montclair, New Jersey.

Dad wore a tie when he went fishing, and was careful to keep his slacks tucked neatly into his waders. No one in the family owned a pair of blue jeans; they were banned along with other "common" indulgences like chewing gum, soft drinks, and any shirt that didn't

The Madam riding sidesaddle in a Hot Springs horse show, mid 1930's.

have to be ironed. Mother rarely wore slacks, and never appeared in public without lipstick and rouge. Dinner was a coat-and-tie event, no children invited (I was fed in the kitchen, thank goodness). The tie-and-kitchen rule was relaxed only if we went to the picnic grounds at the river. No ties there. And no hot dogs, hamburgers, pickles, relish or other pedestrian foods, either. Giant lamb chops, or a *chateaubriand*, were cooked over the fire, vegetables and perhaps a *soufflé* were whisked down from the kitchen, and, of course, my grandfather's piano was trucked down and placed on the portable dance floor. He was indeed a wonderful musician, and before the evening was out, everyone would gather 'round for a few choruses of *Boola Boola*, a song he had written in 1900 when he was a senior at Yale.

Steeple chase near Bacova, late 1920's.

Like the duck press, he got a lot of mileage out of that song, but like a lot of other tales of family glory, it had a hidden side.

A few years ago the family home in Montclair was finally sold. In the process of cleaning out the attic, a box full of documents, books and music was found. The box was the sort used to send laundry back and forth to prep school. This one was used by my Uncle Jack while he was at Hotchkiss in the late 1930's.

Among the documents was a letter written in 1930 by Grandfather to a school girl in Georgia. She had written to Yale University "in regard to the history of the *Boola* Song," and for the first time I realized the authorship of the song was a bit more complex than I had been told. It was written in the fall of 1900. In the letter to "My dear Miss Coleman," Grandfather revealed that two friends, F.M. VanWincklen and A.M. Marchwald, both had a hand in writing the tune "though how much each of us did it is difficult to say." He was helped with the words (yes, there are words; it's not just "*Boola Boola*" over and over, though that's the part that survives) by another classmate, James L. Boyce. "That was on a Friday afternoon, and the next day, Saturday, I got together a group of classmates, taught them the song for the first time. It immediately made a hit and has been sung at Yale ever since."

In spite of its collective authorship, Grandfather got a copyright on the song—no mention of the others—and it became an instant best seller. John Phillip Sousa performed it early in 1901, and the sheet music sold more copies than any other song for six months after it was published.

No one in the family had mentioned anything about Messrs. Van Wincklen, Marchwald and Boyce. That was a surprise to me, but only the first of three *Boola* surprises.

When *Boola* was about to turn 100, I wrote an article describing the song's history as I know it for the Yale Alumni Magazine, relying heavily on the details in the long-hidden letter to the schoolgirl in Midville, Georgia. I thought it might have some passing interest to my Yale colleagues, but I did not expect the stir it caused. An attorney called the magazine to say that the *Boola* tune was not original, and was in fact written by two black songwriters well ahead of Grandfather.

In the Coleman letter, Grandfather says "the tune is not altogether original with us, but was undoubtedly adapted from some other song. But we were unable to definitely designate this song, although later on we did discover that there had been published a song which at that time was out of print, called "*La Hula Boola*" (sic) and the air was quite similar but the tune was different."

Fascinating! Did he know when he got the copyright that it may have at least been awfully close to the other song? More to the point: did he know it was the work of black writers? Given his attitude toward African American people, it's not hard to imagine him simply dismissing the legitimacy of their work.

"Boola Boola" sheet music, 1901. No question about who wrote it.

Whether he knew it or not, what an amazing irony that he got a lifetime of credit out of what may have been the work of two black songsters writing only twenty or so years after slavery ended.

Grandfather's
"Struggle Stick," made about 1897. His
"invention" was part
Porch Fiddle, part Stumph Fiddle.

But there is one more twist to the tale. In response to the article, I heard from Mr. Marchwald's son-in-law who sent me a picture of Grandfather and Mr. Marchwald at a 1930 Yale function. The caption described the two as co-authors of *Boola*. He said it was a rare acknowledgment, and his father-in-law, even though he remained friendly with Grandfather throughout his life, always resented not being more widely recognized as a co-author of *Boola*. Even when they socialized and Grandfather did his inevitable *Boola* performance, he never tipped his bowler to his friend.

Until the end, that is. Just days before Pop died he called Mr. Marchwald and apologized for hogging the credit all those many years. One can imagine the emotion both men must have experienced in that exquisitely painful but healing moment. Of all the little hidden details about my family I have been able to mine over the years, the image of my dying grandfather on the phone making amends with his old friend is one of the most powerful.

Also in the attic box were dozens of marches and other songs Grandfather wrote. Many were written for several different instruments, each copied in Pop's careful hand, complete with detailed notes about how the tunes were to be played. There goes another family myth: he could play anything on the piano, but always claimed he couldn't read a note of music. All by ear, so help me!

Another of my most vivid memories of Grandfather—especially at the elaborate picnics by the river—was his playing the "Struggle Stick," an instrument he claims to have invented while at Yale. It was a sort of one-man band, a stout stick with a Chinese drum in the middle, a bass piano wire stretched top to bottom with a wooden bridge on the drum giving tremendous resonance to the bass, and three brass symbols pierced by several rattling nuts and bolts. Tambourine rattles were mounted on two short horizontal wooden pegs to complete the instrument. He played it by simultaneously bouncing it on the floor with his left hand and plucking the bass string and hitting the drum with his right hand. The big trick was managing the left hand since it had to both bounce the stick and slide a bottle neck up and down the bass string to change the notes.

He got a tremendous amount of music out of the Struggle Stick. But I am not the only one who remembers his performances. The daughter of one of the farm hands I mentioned earlier—Dottie, the girl who never met or even remembers speaking to my grandmother—told me that every year on her and her twin sister's birthday Grandfather came to their house and played *Happy Birthday Dear Dottie and Doris* on the Struggle Stick.

"It was like Santa Claus for us," Dottie said. "We all hoped he would come, and he never disappointed us." She remembers Grandfather singing and playing while they all marched around the house behind him. Like Dottie, that is my favorite sort of Grandfather memory: the jolly musician having fun away from my sour, killjoy grandmother.

But he didn't invent the Struggle Stick. Again, while trying to get my facts straight I looked into the origin of the instrument and found it to be a chimera of two other instruments: the southern slave's "Porch Fiddle," and an east European (Czech) miner's instrument now called the "Stumph Fiddle."

The slave's variety was simply a wire secured tightly from the wall of a porch to the floor, and played as Grandfather did, by sliding a piece of glass or a small knife blade up and down the wire while plucking it like a stand-up bass. The Stumph Fiddle has a center pole with a tunable string stretched over a tambourine, and is played by hitting the string and tambourine with a drumstick.

The only reason I belabor the details of the Struggle Stick is because such a to-do was made over the idea that Grandfather *invented* the darn thing. It wasn't enough that he played the hell out of it, there always had to be that extra show-off touch, the little embellishment to make sure you were *really* impressed. And like so much of what he (and the others) did, his accomplishments were real, and the need to enhance them was unnecessary.

One example of a genuine and unique talent he didn't need to exaggerate was his ability to play baseball. After he got tossed out of

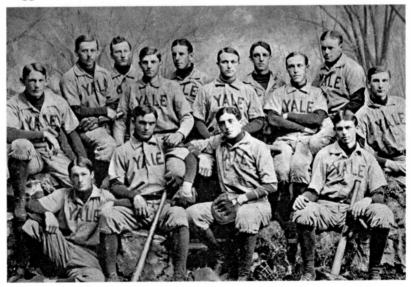

Yale baseball team, 1900. Grandfather with catcher's mitt.

Andover in 1895 (I never found out why), he returned to Richmond and enrolled in the University of Richmond. He was the catcher on their baseball team, and in the spring of his sophomore year they played the touring Yale team. The Yale coach was so impressed he recruited him on the spot.

When he got to New Haven in the fall of 1897 he was two years older than most of his classmates—thus the "Pop" nickname. He played catcher for Yale, roomed with the Captain, and surrounded himself with baseball players and musicians.

After he left Yale, he played catcher in a semi-pro baseball league until a foul tip fractured his larynx. After that he was a practice catcher for the New York Highlanders pitching squad.[3] He had a powerful arm, and could throw to the second baseman without standing up. It was almost impossible to steal a base on Pop Hirsh.

When Grandfather graduated in the spring of 1901 he seemed to be riding the crest of a perfect wave. *Boola Boola* was a hit song, he had a contract to play baseball in the minors poised for a career with a major league team, and his notoriety coupled with his college connections gave him a powerful leg up in the business community.

But the view from the top of the wave was different. Lying invisibly just under the surface directly in his path was an enormous hungry shark waiting to tear him to shreds. No ordinary shark, this one only ate Jews.

Grandfather grew up in a large and prosperous Jewish community in Richmond, Virginia. His grandfather, Abraham, emigrated from Bavaria early in the 19th Century fleeing a crushing anti-Semitic system that permitted only one son in each family to marry, rigidly limited livelihood options, and routinely pressed males into extensive unpaid service fighting micro-wars for feudal princes. Abraham, his wife and a sister came to Richmond with a group of friends, assimilated, and quickly prospered in a free country where ambition and competition put everyone on an equal footing.

Uncomfortable worshiping in a Portuguese-speaking Sephardic temple, the Bavarian cohort founded its own German-speaking temple and school. Beth Ahaba quickly grew to become an established intellectual center and magnet for Jewish scholars from Europe and the rest of the young nation. Abraham's son, Samson, married Amelia Millhiser, daughter of Moses Millhiser, an extremely successful lumber and retail merchant, and President of the Beth Ahaba Congregation from 1867 to his death in 1898.

Samson's brother Herman died in the Civil War, and the family's home and businesses were destroyed by Grant's army. But they rebuilt and within a decade were again prosperous and comfortable in Richmond society.

Herman's death was devastating, more so because he was killed by his own troops while returning to the front line from a pass. His parents thought he had been murdered but an investigation ruled his death an accident. Unconvinced, they buried Herman with a silver dagger in his hand to forever protect him from surprise attack.

Assimilated Jewish communities in the 1800's were generally unthreatened by flagrant anti-Semitism, although smoldering bias was always a background fact of life. After the Civil War, for example, insurance companies would not sell risk policies to Jews in Richmond and other selected communities. Toward the end of the century anti-immigration sentiment surged, its focus mainly fastened on the Italians and Irish, but increasingly on the influx of desperately poor, uneducated East European Jews. Established Jewish families suddenly felt the heat pushing some to abandon Judaism altogether. A surprising number themselves became intensely anti-Semitic. In 1894 Grandfather dropped his birth name "Abraham" in favor of the more generic "Allan," an acknowledgement of ethnic discomfort that cannot have gone unnoticed by Moses Millhiser and other observant members of the family. Apparently it didn't matter to Allan and his immediate family. It was the start of their determined effort to forge a new identity in the world of Aryan opportunity.

Grandfather's experience at Yale certainly reinforced the need for metamorphosis. Being Mr. Popular, a songster, athlete and talented engineer wasn't enough to overcome the Jewish obstacle. Don't even *imagine* getting into Skull and Bones.

Beyond college there was the ugly reality that anti-Semitism could brush aside his accomplishments, force him into a more traditional, stereotyped Jewish enterprise, or send him back to the family's retail and the lumber business in Richmond. True, he certainly would have prospered, but Grandfather's social and business ambitions lay in another direction.

Something must change and it had to be both immediate and radical. It was time to molt and leave the family's Jewish skin in Richmond.

A family's identity and values usually evolve slowly, tempered over time by the personalities and countless experiences of succeeding generations. But sometimes an event or a particularly influential figure catches the family at a vulnerable moment and causes a tectonic shift permanently redirecting the family's persona. Though dramatic when it happens, time and events quickly obscure those changes. Only rarely does one get to look back over a considerable time span to see the moment and understand the reason for an abrupt turn, one powerful enough to define—and subtly confuse—generations to follow.

But when Grandfather left Yale he and his parents jettisoned their Jewish history, papered over their heritage, and moved to Montclair, New Jersey as newly-minted Unitarians. The New Model was born.

Part of the reason they were able to so completely vanish their history was the relatively small size of the immediate family. Grandfather came to Montclair with his parents and two older sisters, all on board with the change. The only other close relative was Samson's married sister who lived in Baltimore. They already weren't close, and after the Unitarian transformation they maintained little more than polite contact. In 1906 Grandfather married my thoroughly Protestant grandmother, and from then on no mention was made of anything Jewish.

The family secret was so deeply buried that I grew up completely oblivious to it, aware only that Jews were in the dumpster along with all the others the family defined as undesirable. The idea that anyone would think we were or ever had been Jewish was simply preposterous, a slanderous affront.

I was keenly aware of Father's hair-trigger sensitivity to the notion people might assume "Hirsh" to be a Jewish name. Many times I heard him angrily proclaim the Gospel of Dad: *Hirsch* is Jewish, *Hirsh* is not. Amen.

The family fever over the name ran so high there was a move to change it to Hughson, a good waspy name from my grandmother's uncontaminated side of the family. The idea surfaced again and again, and finally, in the late 1940's, the necessary legal process was started. It was dropped when Grandfather became ill.

I managed to get through my entire education—including medical school—without seriously thinking about the Jewish question. When I was thirteen, without any warning, I was suddenly compelled to attend Confirmation class at the Episcopal church. No one said why, so I suffered it and was "confirmed." Not only did it make absolutely no sense to me either spiritually or as a social necessity, but it threatened to ruin every weekend because somehow being confirmed also meant one had to attend church on a regular basis. And that wasn't all: I also had to sing in the choir. Happily, I was immediately pitched out for throwing a small firecracker from the upper to the lower choir loft before practice one evening. I went home and told Father thinking this might get me shot.

He was reading his newspaper and when I said, "Dad, there's something I have to tell you," he grunted, "What?" without lowering the paper.

Speaking to him through the classified section of the *Newark Evening News* I said, "Mr. Thomas threw me out of the choir."

"Why?" he asked, still hidden behind the paper screen.

"I threw a baby-waker out of the choir loft. I didn't think Mr. Thomas was there yet."

"That was pretty stupid," he said through the paper.

I waited but nothing happened. Then I asked a real question. "Dad, do you believe in God?"

He moved his hands slightly closer together and the paper formed a shallow V exposing the top part of his face. He stared at me briefly and said, "That's something you'll have to figure out for yourself." He snapped the paper back and his face disappeared. Thinking back, it was probably the best piece of advice he ever gave me.

After I finished my internship I decided to go into psychiatry, and began my residency and psychoanalysis at the same time. Both piqued my interest in family history, and still not fastened on the Jewish piece, I went to work interviewing relatives and looking through old photo albums. Getting information on my mother's side was an easy matter. There was a good deal in print and everyone was happy to talk about Walkers and Scudders.

There was also plenty of information available on the Hughsons. But when the spotlight was on the Hirsh side it was a different matter. Everything before 1901 was a black hole, and it obviously made some people anxious—even angry—to be pressed for details.

My normally quiet analyst was roused to say, "It sounds like you've got a Jew in the woodpile." One trip to the Virginia Archives and a detour to Beth Ahaba easily showed me the Jewish connection. I wanted to tell my father, of course, but I knew the news would not make him happy, so I carefully presented it in private (on the beach in front of his Palm Beach home), and in the most non-provocative way I could imagine.

The instant I said the word "Jewish" he exploded. "It's a f~g lie!" he screamed. He stormed off the beach without hearing any of the details. He couldn't tolerate it, and barely spoke to me over the next two years.

Having secrets, especially industrial-strength ones, requires supporting fables and stories to make sure the New Model is properly and seamlessly explained to succeeding generations. In our family *Life As We Know It* began in 1901. Grandfather came out of college, went into business, and was instantly successful. Getting clocked in the throat by a foul tip took him out of baseball; no big deal, he was too busy with his new business to play professionally anyway. In 1906 he married and lived a long, happy life full of music, horses, dogs and river-side picnics.

It took a considerable amount of careful digging to uncover the true details of the Hirsh family. It was obvious after my disastrous encounter with Father on the beach that the family line was hardened around non-Jewish fables—names and dates deleted— a process that began well before Grandfather left college. And even though I was then an adult, a physician about to start a career, and a man looking at his family history seriously and with every good intention, none of that had enough weight to break through the wall of resistance.

My uncle Allan, the oldest of the four boys, was an ill-tempered snob, emotionally and physically abusive to his two children, and he had no interest in talking to me about the past. I had to try, but he angrily dismissed me. Interestingly, the last time I saw him was in 1997, a year after Father died. The box of *Boola Boola* documents had been found in the Montclair house and Allan had graciously (and uncharacteristically) let me look at them, though he was reluctant to part with any of them. I managed to talk him out of about half of the stuff, thanked him, then brought up the thirty-year-old unanswered question about the family's Jewish history. We both knew I already had the answers, there was no escaping that. I just wanted to see how he felt about it now that his life was drawing to a close.

I posed it as gently as possible saying that Father had rejected the idea of a Jewish background. "Perhaps he didn't know," I said. "Did you?"

Allan looked at me and after a long pause said angrily, "Of course I knew. What difference does it make?"

"It was a lot to live with," I said. "Your parents put an emotional burden on all of you." He flicked his hand as if brushing away a fly, got up and left the room. I never saw him again.

Malcolm was a little easier but no more informative. Yes, no, maybe. They could have been, I don't think so, there were rumors. Thanks, Malc.

Sitting with my grandmother one Sunday morning, notebook in hand, I asked directly if the Hirshs weren't, in fact, a Jewish family? She looked me dead in the eye and said "No." They may have had some Jewish relatives somewhere, but my grandfather and his direct relatives definitely were not Jewish.

"They were from Bavaria," she said. It was like talking to the Coneheads.

But here is the real story. When they came to Montclair, Samson and Amelia built an enormous home with a formal garden, and filled the place with stuffed birds and curios from their world travels, including a Buddhist shrine hauled back from Burma. In 1901 Samson and Son went into the banking business in New York City. Everything was looking good.

Unfortunately, there was also an economic downturn in 1901, their business faltered, and they were forced to try an alternative venture.

Enter Old Man Merriweather, new husband of Grandfather's sister, Florine, and owner of a patent on the "lock joint." The lock joint became the focus of the family's new prosperity so it's worth a minute to describe it. Picture a piece of concrete pipe about 18 inches long and a foot or so in diameter, then split it in half length-wise. The lock joint was molded into the edges of the split halves so they could be snapped in place around a dock piling then slid down the post into the water. Coupled sections were piled on top of each other until the entire wooden post was wrapped in a protective concrete casing safe from trauma, rot and barnacles.

It was a good idea that essentially went nowhere, and by 1904 the company was teetering on failure. To make matters worse, Old Man Merriweather had taken a shine to his secretary, Miss Havemeyer, and the two had run off together.

That's when the light went off in Grandfather's head. He found Merriweather and made an enticing offer: your patent for an easy, all-expenses paid exit from the twin inconveniences of marriage to his sister and business. Grandfather got the patent, Merriweather got his divorce, and he and Miss Havemeyer got each other. The latter part turned out to be the worst part of the bargain. According to Grandfather, one of them had syphilis, soon they both had it, and they ended their lives in an asylum for the hopelessly demented. True or not, it was *said* to be so, and that *made* it so.

Grandfather's out-of-the-box idea was to put the lock joint on the ends of the concrete pipe, creating a nearly leak-proof, inexpensive alternative to steel and cast iron water pipe. Using relatively cheap concrete and a series of patented cores, wrappings and coatings, the Lock Joint Pipe Company became hugely successful.

But getting LJP from idea to production required an infusion of cash, fifty thousand dollars more than they had, to be exact. So they turned to Samson's brother-in-law, Gus Millhiser, at that time one of the wealthiest men in Virginia.

I learned the details of the meeting in the 1960's from Ross Millhiser, Gus's great-nephew and President of Phillip Morris, shortly after my disastrous confrontation with Father over my family research. According to Ross, Gus was furious with Samson for turning his back on the family's heritage. In the end he loaned them the money but said he would *never* do so again. When he died fourteen years later he left his sister Amelia \$200,000—no small amount in 1916—but the bulk of his estate went to his brother, Clarence.

Armed with Gus' money and Merriweather's patent, Grandfather formed the company in 1905. Samson dropped out of the picture to tend his roses, and Grandfather pushed ahead with the novel idea of concrete water pipe. He hired a nucleus of young engineers from his Yale contacts, and within two years made enough money to pay Gus back. Eventually the company became a global enterprise, traded on the NYSE, and made a considerable fortune for its founder.

All of the old timers I have talked to who knew Grandfather agree he was both a brilliant engineer and a powerful manager of people. He was a good listener, impatient with digression, and quick to master details of complex engineering projects. He was demanding but fair, and generated tremendous loyalty among his employees. He was also dead certain about his instincts and intimidating in bidding and negotiations.

His office in East Orange, New Jersey, was set up to reflect both his personality and business style. It was a huge, high-ceiling room furnished like a men's club. At one end couches and easy chairs were grouped around a walk-in fireplace. Horse and hunting scene prints, Punch and Vanity Fair drawings hung on the walls, and there were large oriental rugs on the parquet floor. At the other end, perched on a slightly elevated section of floor, his desk sat alone in the middle of the room, a few chairs beside and behind but none directly in front. The room smelled of wood smoke and cigars.

Everyone in the room stood or sat literally in front and below Grandfather's stage.

Another point of agreement among those who worked for him had to do with hiring. Grandfather personally screened every applicant, and in the entire time he and his two older sons ran the company, they never hired a Jew.

With his business well under way Grandfather turned to the issue of marriage. According to Grandmother she had to battle through numerous admirers. Just what he saw in the Madam, given her rotten personality, is unclear. To be sure she had the right credentials: daughter of wealthy WASP's, self-confident, musical, well-traveled and a horse lover. Moreover (and perhaps as important as anything else) she appeared unconcerned about his Jewish background and as ready as he was to move forward as a vaguely Christian family.

Above all, though, she was—like Grandfather—acquisitive, and the Jewish thing would have been seen not as an issue of principle but instead as something one gets over, like the embarrassment of having an uncle who robbed a bank. Forget it, it's his problem, not ours.

The wedding took place in the fall of 1906 in Montclair, catered by Delmonico's. Many of the Jewish relatives came, though Uncle Gus regretted. Having found his attempts to select a gift "defeated" he sent a check instead, "Knowing you will be able to put it to its best use." His fatherly letter encouraged the newlyweds to let their "lips reach the fountain from which flows the stimulus to redoubled effort," whatever that means. He urged tireless devotion to each other and the family at large. Affectionately, Uncle Gus.

All-in-all it was a gracious effort given the confrontation between Grandfather, Samson and Gus just two years before. His

Three of Grandfather's lady friends from his undergraduate days...

Fifi

49

Beatrice

One look at Mary Louise Hughson Reid (above), his future mother-in-law,
should have sent Grandfather back to FiFi.

The Madam as a child about 1887,
her firm jaw already set.

Her formal portrait—
a gift to Grandfather—
in 1902.

wedding message, however obscure, was a lot better than my father's advice to me on the eve of my own wedding. Seemingly out of nowhere he said he wanted to talk to me and led me into the coat room at the Princeton Inn.

"Your mother says I should talk to you about marriage. Okay, here it is. Just remember one thing: all women are irrational." He left the room before I could open my mouth.

Sadly, Grandfather died before I ever had a chance to have anything more than a superficial conversation with him—with one exception. My memories of him all center in one way or another on entertainment, either on his baseball diamond or at the piano. He always played *Boola Boola*, *Eenie meenie minie mo* (*Catch a nigger by the toe*), and *Dixie*. One day when I was about six, I asked him why *Dixie* was such a favorite. He was obviously passionate about the tune and I was curious.

He stood up from the piano and said, "I'll show you." We left the house and walked to his parent's house three blocks away. Samson and Amelia were long gone and his widowed sister Estelle lived alone—except for servants—in the huge house. We walked in without even saying hello to Estelle (she was stone deaf and unless you stood directly in front of her and screamed she had no clue you were there). We walked up the long flight of stairs to the second floor, more stairs to the third floor and up a final flight to the vast attic. Grandfather found an old steamer trunk, dragged it under a light hanging on a long cord and opened it. Inside were piles of what I remember as curtains and table cloths. He piled them up on the dusty floor until he got to the bottom of the trunk. With considerable care he lifted out two large folded flags. He slowly unfurled them and held each up for me to see. They were so large that even with his arms spread widely apart only about half of each flag was exposed. They were both in poor repair, full of small round holes, tears and burn marks. While I didn't know it at the time, the two flags were the Confederate battle flag (the one we most often

53

The Hirsh family in Montclair, New Jersey, 1928. Back row: Great Grandmother, Amelia Millhiser Hirsh; my father, Philip, Sr.; Grandfather, Allan (Abraham) M. Hirsh, Sr; uncle, Allan, Jr. Front row (left to right) John (Jack), the Madam and Malcolm.

associate with the South), and the lesser known Stars and Bars, the official flag of the Confederacy. He told me they had flown over the family's home on Franklin Street when Richmond fell.

"And that's why I love *Dixie*," he said with sad, almost scary, forcefulness. He folded the flags, put them carefully back in the trunk, pushed the trunk back into its dusty corner, and we walked back to his house. I had no idea at the time what in the world he was talking about, but his uncharacteristically somber, even gloomy, mood told me this was an important moment. I treated it seriously, tried to look like I really did grasp the lesson, and hoped desperately he wouldn't quiz me about it on the way back. He didn't; in fact, I don't think much was said at all.

After Aunt Estelle died in 1956, Malcolm donated the flags to the museum at Washington and Lee University.

Another of Grandfather's repeat performances took place on the baseball diamond he built next to his house, usually with a group of guests who gathered to watch his signature catcher's trick: throwing the ball to the second baseman from the squat position. With Father on the mound, Uncle Allan at second, and some guest at bat, he would take the pitch and in an instant snap his arm, throwing the ball with such speed and flat trajectory that Father would have to dive to the ground to avoid getting hit in the face. The ball always landed a foot or so off the ground on the first base side of the bag. It was great and dependable theater.

When people asked him how he developed that trick, he couldn't simply say something about working at his father's lumberyard. No, he said it came from "throwing rocks at niggers" when he was a kid in Richmond. He wasn't bashful about his racism.

There was another game he liked to play on his private baseball field, one that only involved the two older boys, Allan and my father, Philip. It was called "burn-out." The two younger sons,

Jack and Malcolm, refused to play, and were both ridiculed by their father and brothers for their non-competitive nature.

Burn-out was a two-person game. Starting 10-15 feet from each other, one would throw the ball as hard as possible trying to back the other up. The exchange continued until one player was forced to back over a line 40-50 feet behind. Guess who won Burnout every time?

As a kid I never played Burnout with Father, but I was forced to play a nasty variant called (what else?) Nigger Baby. Everyone else called it "Spud," a Dodgeball variant played as a group. One person threw a ball into the air, called a number, and everyone scattered in different directions. The kid whose number was called caught the ball and yelled "Stop!" freezing the other players. The one with the ball took three giant steps toward the nearest kid and threw the ball at him. You could move one foot, duck and twist any way to avoid being hit. If you were hit, you had an "S;" if the thrower missed, he got the "S." Then came the "P" and so on until someone had "SPUD" and was eliminated. Last one in the game wins. End of game, let's do it again.

Nigger Baby, like Burnout, was a two-person game: just Father and me. There was never any doubt whose number was going to be called. When I threw the ball, I rarely got very far, and three of Father's giant steps put him within inches of me. All he had to do was drop the ball on my head and I had an "N." When he threw the ball up it went into the ionosphere, and by the time I got control of it, Father was across the neighbor's yard behind a tree. It took exactly six throws for me to be "NIGGER." If the game had ended there, it wouldn't have been more than humiliating. But it didn't. The loser (guess who?) had to stand facing the garage wall while the winner (guess who?) stood back 10-15 feet and threw the ball three times as hard as he liked at the back of the loser. I did my very best to avoid Father on Saturday mornings—his favorite time to play the game.

When I was just a toddler I was oblivious to the notion of the players, their rules, or the way responsibility was triaged. But during that first summer of memory, the effect of going back and forth between the servant-world and the parent-world started to impact my behavior more dramatically. It was a two-world system, and I was the only one in the entire organization who moved freely between the two.

Increasingly, I came to prefer the company of people my parents hardly noticed and certainly did not value beyond their function as servants. If they had realized at the time what was happening, or the consequences the split system would have on the direction my life was to take, they would have been horrified. But they were protected from that insight by a thick veneer of denial based on the assumption that the servant group existed only to reflect the greater glory of the family. Having no group identity or individual worth beyond what the family gave them, there was no risk they would teach me anything but the family catechism.

The self-assurances made about servant loyalty extended as well to the community. Every farmer, blacksmith, shopkeeper and county clerk was considered a "local." Some, because of a skill or talent, were respected, but respect—no matter how strong—never translated into upward status. Once a local, always a local. Their role was to be submissive appendages happily subordinating their lives and saying their lines in collective validation of the system.

In spite of being clearly dependent on the employees and good will of the community, a core family assumption was that the opposite was true: they needed us, not the other way around. Even the notion of shared or reciprocal dependence was far too radical to enter their minds.

The concept of "place" helped enfranchise the entire operation. One had to know his or her place in the system. Our place was on top of the pile, theirs was in varying proportion somewhere below, grateful for the opportunity to work for such rich and fun-loving people. Working for the family was a privilege, something to brag about. Offering employment was a *noblesse oblige* exercise in community responsibility.

The fortunate hirelings received parsimonious wages, and on special occasions (like Christmas), a token gift or bonus—perhaps an extra day off or maybe a discarded suit. Otherwise, the staff were like children: better seen than heard, always on their toes to be correct and obedient. When Grandmother forgot to put the parking brake on her station wagon, and it rolled down the hill into the duck pond, it was treated as a big joke. Wasn't it funny to see the Chrysler nose down in the mud? Ha! Ha!

But if a maid dropped a dinner plate, she could be fired on the spot, and Grandmother would stay hot over it for days. When the husband of one of the maids died and she requested two weeks off to recover, with great reluctance she was given one week. Still weeping when she came back, she was told in no uncertain terms to shape up or turn in her apron. That, after more than twenty years of service.

Everyone in the family, as well as their guests, played by the same rules. They could be at a horse show, dancing in the Crystal Room at the Homestead, bobbing in the Warm Springs pools, or sitting on the porch sipping mint juleps from silver goblets. It didn't make a bit of difference, it was always the same. Servants, of course, were invisible, unless the dessert was late or the chauffeur was caught without his gloves.

Occasionally, there were hints of exception to the invisibility rule. After years and years of service, I sensed that my mother became very close to some of the staff, particularly Alice. Forced to endure the Madam at close range over protracted periods of time, particularly in the summer at the farm where she had no allies, it's not surprising Mother would turn to someone so intimately involved with the system for a little support.

Alice always seemed oblivious and unruffled by the Madam's frequent tirades. So when Mother was about to explode with frustration over my grandmother's behavior, or my father's lack of willingness to take up for her in one of the frequent family squabbles, it's easy to imagine her turning to Alice. I wasn't privy to the conversations, to be sure, but I'd bet my hat Mother wanted to know how in the world Alice did it. How could she remain so placid, so seemingly above it all? What's your trick, Alice?

Acknowledging feelings or discussing private matters with an employee was verboten, and I never saw it as a child. This created problems for me, because like any youngster cared for by an intensely nurturing group, I expressed my affection in return. But when I was caught giving a maid a hug, I was scolded.

To the servants I was Master Philip, even when my parents were not around. I could call them by their first names, but it didn't work the other way around. It didn't take very long for me to figure out that when the family was out of earshot I could relax and say what I wanted. But when parents or grandparents were about, Master Philip held his tongue, and kept his distance, increasingly aware of the peril of showing preference for the wrong group. I also became skillful in managing my behavior to appear like a good family apprentice eager to join the firm. Since I only spent about 20% of my time with family, it didn't take much energy to stay clear of trouble.

When we arrived in the early part of the summer of 1941, I met my new nursemaid, Miss Hite, a young woman who was my summer companion, teacher and supporter for three years. She was white, a rider, and newly married. Like Alice—but without the long period of practice time—she had the ability to both tolerate and politely resist the Madam.

Much later in life it came as a shock to realize there were people who simply weren't impressed or intimidated by the family parade. They either didn't deal with us at all, or limited their involvement to a particular area and paid no attention to the rest. Talking (through letters) about it years later, Miss Hite said she genuinely enjoyed her job, but told Mother early on that she would not wear a silly uniform, and was prepared to leave the instant anyone tried to bully her. Being a rider, she was too rare a find to lose, though the battle of the overalls nearly did it.

One of Miss Hite's first suggestions was to get me a pair of bib overalls. When I wasn't wearing miniature jodhpurs, I wore frilly shorts like some cartoon caricature of the rich sissy. Since I spent a lot of time in the barns, and loved to "help" the men muck out the stalls, it seemed obvious to Miss Hite that I should be more appropriately dressed. She recalled the Madam's explosion when Mother sided with the overalls idea. Apparently, the Madam only gave in when Miss Hite headed for the door, and I got my first real man's clothing.

Since riding instruction was to be the focus of my summers, two ponies were bought, one to ride, the other to pull my pony cart. The cart was a two-person wicker cart with a tiny door in the stern. The theory was that every proper horseman had to know how to control his steed both as a mount and as a draught animal. Every day began with a riding lesson, and in the afternoon a cart ride to Webb's, a general store about four miles up the dirt road toward Warm Springs. The round trip, with stops, took most of the afternoon.

The first pony trauma was over names. I was told that since they were mine, I was to name them. So with everyone staring at me I had to instantly come up with two gender-correct names. The snag was, I didn't know if they were male or female. The cart pony came with the name Dasher, so I simply declared I liked it. End of story.

But the other one needed a name, so I bravely found the middle ground, covered all bets, and named the pony Jim Sally. It was taken as a sign of early humor, not ignorance, and I escaped any ridicule.

Proudly showing off my brand new overalls.

Miss Hite was an expert horsewoman, but more importantly, she knew I was scared to death to be mounted on Jim Sally. To admit fear to the family was out of the question, but entirely reasonable to Miss Hite, who always kept a firm grip on the head lead. Still, it took the better part of two summers for me to become comfortable and able to ride off-lead.

I was always supposed to wear a proper riding outfit right down to the out-sized riding crop held with the correct number of fingers in the correct hand at the correct angle. Back straight. Watch those toes, don't look like a duck on horseback.

But when the parent figures were absent, I rode in my overalls, no crop. Screw the toes.

The pony cart was even better because driving it was not a big trick, and Miss Hite was right there in case Dasher shied or tried to run. Better still, it gave us hours of alone time to talk and sing.

On Jim Sally, almost three. Note the outsized riding crop.

Miss Hite had a sweet voice and knew a slew of mountain songs and Scottish-English ballads. We clomped down the lane singing *Jimmy Crack Corn, Old Dan Tucker, It Ain't Gunna Rain No More,* and *Bonnie Barbara Allen.*

We sometimes marched to the barn singing *When Johnny Comes Marching Home*; that is, until my grandfather caught us and banned the tune. It was a "Yankee" song and therefore inappropriate for a grandchild of the South—even if he did live in New Jersey.[4]

My favorite song, by far, was *The Poor Old Slave.* The tune was so slow and sweet it made you want to swing your head and shoulders with each two-word trochee phrase. It was sad, too, but in a hopeful kind of way. Even a little kid who didn't have a clue what a slave was could feel it; that is, if he had the right singing partner.

On Jim Sally in the middle of the Jackson River.

On Jim Sally at four, showing a little more confidence.

63

'Tis just one year ago today, that I remember well.

I sat down by Nelly's side, and a story she did tell.

'Twas 'bout a poor unhappy slave, that lived for many a year.

But now he's dead, and in his grave, no master does he fear.

The poor old slave has gone to rest

We know that he is free.

Disturb him not, but let him rest

'Way down in Tennessee!

She took my arm, we walked along, in to an open field.

And there she paused to breathe a while, then to his grave did steal.

She sat down by that little mound, and softly whispered there,

Come to me, father, 'tis thy child, then gently dropped a tear.

The poor old slave has gone to rest,

We know that he is free.

Disturb him not, but let him rest

'Way down in Tennessee!

Sometimes she sang the second line of the chorus:

We know that he is free, free-free

And sometimes she sped the chorus up and sang it in a kind of pig-Latin, each repeat more complex and seemingly garbled than the last. It always made me laugh, and I don't think a day went by when we didn't sing *The Poor Old Slave.*

We had our favorite stopping spots, mossy cushioned places shaded by huge old trees where—if you looked carefully—you could see the wood fairy dens shaded by their toadstool umbrellas. You could chew a minty teaberry leaf or weave pine needle corrals for

Getting ready for a cart ride with Dasher and Miss Hite.

the tiny woodland sheep the fairies kept. And it was important to find an empty acorn shell to push into the moss in the middle of a corral to catch raindrops to water the sheep.

Sometimes we found rain lizards under the moss. Some were bright red and very shy (that's why they are red: they are embarrassed to be seen in public). And there were bigger black ones covered with dozens of ivory-white spots. They were slow and didn't mind being handled (they were the fairies' house painters—that's how come they were covered with paint spots).

Sometimes when we were walking we went up Hellgrammite Run to catch yet another kind of lizard, this one liked to hide under flat rocks in the little creek that snaked down the deep hollow. These guys were coal-black, and so slippery you couldn't possibly hold one unless you knew the secret way to catch them. Moving very slowly, you form a fingers-together shallow cup with your left hand, and carefully put it on the ground about an inch in front of the lizard's nose. Then bring your right hand up behind the lizard and touch his tail. A split second later he will explode forward up your finger ramp. If you are quick enough and time it just right, you snap your hand closed and he's trapped in the palm cave. If you try to grab him, he'll slime out between your fingers no matter how hard you squeeze.

The other lizard we caught was actually a newt. Newts live in ponds so to catch them we took off our shoes and waded into the lily pads. Miss Hite had the quickest hands around. She could catch newts, frogs, turtles and sometimes a beautiful, thin Green Snake sunning itself on a log.

She taught me two fabulous pond tricks; I've taught both to my children and grandchildren.

The first is How To Catch a Turtle. You sneak slowly along the edge of the pond, one careful step at a time. That way you can get on top of the turtles sunning themselves along the edge before they see you and dive. The secret fact is they always swim to the bottom and make for the deep water in a straight line. All you have to do is jump in the water about three feet from the bank, one foot on each side of his escape line. You don't even have to see him, just jump and with both hands grab the bottom between your legs. If you know Miss Hite's secret, and time it right, you'll catch him every time.

The second trick is Newt Shocker, as impressive as the turtle jump, but you need a naïve audience to make it work. First, catch a newt and while everyone is admiring its iridescent red spots and tiny green eyes, remark that the Indians used to eat them raw. "They're good, too," you say as you pop it into your mouth. Then pretend a big swallow, and open your mouth wide to show you really did swallow it. While everyone is screaming "He ate it!! He ate it!!" wipe your mouth, but surreptitiously let the critter out from under your tongue where you had it trapped. Palm the newt, then drop it back in the water when no one is looking. Newts aren't slippery, and they don't seem the worse for a brief visit in your mouth.

But don't, if you're a kid, pull this stunt on your mother. I did, and paid dearly. She was so stunned, and my sleight-of-hand was so skillful, she refused to believe I hadn't actually swallowed it. She loaded me in the car to take me to the hospital to have my stomach pumped. Someone pointed out that people ate live goldfish and lived, so I didn't have to go to the hospital. I don't recall how I got out of being punished, but I did. I think my father secretly thought it was funny to see Mother so agitated, and he got me off the hook.

And I definitely didn't rat on Miss Hite.

Another of our games was played out at Webb's store, our almost daily pony cart destination. The store sat on a hill up a dozen or so stone steps. When we clopped to a halt at the foot of the steps, Miss Hite would make a show of getting Dasher tied to the railing and I would bolt up the stairs.

"He's feelin' juberous today, so you just wait for me," she always said in mock frustration. By then I was already up the steps and heading straight for the soft drink cooler. By the time Miss Hite got up the stairs, I had opened a forbidden bottle of Coke and had half of it down.

"Young man, you know you're not allowed to drink that stuff!" "I tried to stop him, Miss Hite, but he was too slick for me." Mr. Webb was in on it, too. Miss Hite paid the nickel, and sometimes we even split a candy bar.

I loved Webb's store. It smelled of wood smoke and country ham. The shelves and glass cases were crowded with penknives, lanterns, twisted ropes of chewing tobacco, ammunition, jars of udder balm, giant metal veterinarian hypodermics, nose rings for pigs and cattle, elastrators, de-horners, long-snout oil cans, pottery, door springs, padlocks, pocket watches and dynamite fuse. Along a side wall, there were cast iron skillets the size of a tractor seat, huge spools of oily-smelling bailing twine, giant salt blocks and wooden bins full of wheat, barley, oats, rye, corn and clover. Along the other wall there were small barrels of nails of every size and type all sold by the pound: roofing nails, staples, wire nails, galvanized nails, giant spikes and little finishing nails. Hams hung along the back wall and slabs of bacon were stacked in the glass-front refrigerator.

Mr. Webb used a long-handled grabbing device to deftly lift items from the tallest shelves. If an item was too heavy, he nudged it off the shelf and caught it one-handed. He never missed.

Webb's was not just a store; it was a gathering place. Folks stopped by even if they didn't need to buy anything. They leaned against the counter or sat on one of the two long wooden benches on either side of the wood stove and talked about the war, the new preacher, the price of oats, or who had just joined the Army. No one took any particular note of me, though sometimes they ribbed me about my pony cart. But it was always good-natured, and nobody seemed to mind me listening in on their conversations.

What could possibly be better? A place to savor forbidden delicacies, hang out with relaxed, good-natured people, and not worry about how I looked or what I said. At the barn I was always watched, and the grooms were careful about what they said in front of me. But at Webb's there were no such rules, and no censors taking notes for my parents. I loved to sit at one end of the worn wooden counter sipping my drink, and listen to Mr. Webb and his customers talk and laugh.

I didn't always understand exactly what they said, but I loved the sound of the words and phrases of their mountain language. It was more like listening to music than conversation. Sadly, virtually no one uses such words any longer. But when I do hear one today, it always sends a happy memory-shiver through me.

Miss Hite taught me a lot of what she called "old-timey" words, holdovers and fragments of Scotish-English and Irish words, as well as more modern words molded to the mountain ear. Not only were the words themselves wonderfully strange and intriguing, but strung together they had a tune-like quality, a rhythm, almost as if a phrase had been sung rather than spoken. Looking into it now, I'm pleased to find that linguists often refer to the unique tuneful quality of Appalachian language.

The language of the mountains came with the first immigrants who made their way from the middle of the East Coast, across Pennsylvania, and down the Shenandoah Valley in the late 17th and early 18th centuries. They were a mix of northern English, Scotish and Protestant Irish—hard-working, hard-drinking Celtics—plus some Rhineland Germans. Germantown quickly became Warm Springs, and the German tongue itself gave way to the language of the land-hungry *yeoman*, people shut out of the possibility of owning land by English gentry who had passed laws to enclose common land for themselves. They spoke the language of Shakespeare, Elizabethan English richly garnished with Middle English, leftovers from the time of Chaucer.[5] Their shared language and regional expressions blended into the dialect of early Appalachia. Even today Appalachian speech is full of the remains of Elizabethan word forms, spelling and grammar.

Some examples:

Emphasis on an added final t as in *clifft* or *killt*

Contractions/Deletions: 'em, they'd

Heavy use of *r* sound as in *far* (fire) or *har* (hair)

Using *a* before verbs as in *a-hunting* and *a-telling*

Personal dative as in *get me a...* or *she wants herself a...*

Middle English use of *done* as in *done forgot* or *done finished*.

Even the word ain't was used in polite circles in England well into the 19th century. It comes from a series of changes to *has not*: *has not—hasnot—hasn't—hain't—ain't*.[6,7]

The similarity between modern words and Appalachian vernacular incorrectly reinforces the impression of lack of education, or frank ignorance. The word *tetchy*, for example, is not a twisted form of "touchy," though both mean irritable. The word comes from the Middle English word *teeche*. Similarly, *et* isn't "eaten" gone astray; it is a verb form that goes back to the 14th Century. *Hisn*, meaning "his," dates from the 15th Century. *Afeared*, and *flummoxed* are two more old words wrongly assumed to be colloquialisms. Double negatives are frowned on in today's world, but were the rule in 16th Century England.[8]

The word *portly* meant handsome, not fat. *Ashamed* meant shy or bashful, not disgraced. A wedding was a *shivaree* or a *serenade*. And a bastard—the born out of wedlock type—was referred to as a *woods colt*.

Words I often heard included Miss Hite's *juberous* which means nervous, jumpy or undecided. A *gritchel* is a suitcase, a *poke* is a bag. (You wouldn't buy a pig in a poke, would you?) You turn your plow horse by calling *gee* (right), or *haw* (left). *Plumb* and *right much* both mean complete and date to the 15th century. A *beal* is an abcess (boil), and *ary* means single. The list is endless.

My favorite (and one that got me in hot water) is a greeting, the way you answer when someone asks how you are today? "Tol'bly peert," you say, meaning "Reasonably well, thank you." I always assumed it to be an amalgam of *tolerably* and *pert*. But *tolable* (also spelled *tollable*) is an old word meaning mediocre, and *peert* is actually "peart," meaning well or healthy.

Then there are dozens of colloquialisms, a mix of 'regular' and older words given special meaning over time, particularly by the way they are pronounced. A *staub*, for example, is what's left in the ground after you cut corn. A *yo* is a female sheep. You're feeling *peak-ed* when you're tired or getting sick. Almost is *prit-near*. "Lord have mercy" is jammed together as "laws-uh-mercy."

Some words have developed special meaning. *Rightly* means really, as in "I don't rightly know." Three of the most frequently used words are *yonder*, *reckon*, and *spell*. Yonder is a measure of distance. Anything that isn't right here is *yonder*, even if it's three valleys away. Where is the tractor? "Up *yonder* to the barn." Or "*Yonder* she sets." Or "*yonder* a-ways." A slightly more specific alternative to yonder is *over to*. "It's *over to* the barn," or "It's *over to* Pocatontas."

Reckon can mean know, guess, calculate or consider, has wide application, and is often used as a negative. "I don't *reckon*" is a more definite version of "I don't rightly know." As a question, it has a what-do-you-think quality: "You *reckon* it'll rain 'fore we git this hay up?" It's also an alternative to "yes." *Reckon* shaves a bit off the hard affirmative quality of "yes," but doesn't demote it all the way down to "I guess." Are you going to the 4-H fair? "I *reckon* so," meaning I plan to, but it's possible something else could get in the way.

Spell means time, as in "set a *spell*," or "it's been a *spell* since it rained." It has an understood indefinite quality. Everyone knows how long a spell is, but no one can define it in hours or days.

To my family mountain language was yet another sign of ignorance, and grated their ear every bit as much as mountain music. Since the people who spoke it were little more than morons, how in the world could you suggest their language is nuanced, lyrical, or even remotely interesting in any historical sense? Absurd!!

My parents and grandparents both harped on the idea that "locals" were incapable of normal speech, and always (to use their favorite summarizing put-down) "butchered the King's English." It's one of my favorite ironies. In fact, they were using the Queen's English, and doing it rather well. The King's English was actually German. The Hanoverian Georges of most of the 18th century were more at home speaking German than English. George I and II were also Electors of Hanover in Germany—thus the large number of Rhinelanders who faced the same problems of owning land as their yeoman cousins in England, Scotland and Ireland.

But those subtleties were lost on my family who rarely let facts get in the way of their favorite prejudice.

It was another lesson I had to learn the hard way. I announced myself "tol'bly peert" one morning in front of my grandparents. They blasted me for talking "hillbilly,"[9] and demanded to know where I had picked up such trash talk.

I played dumb, looked contrite and promised not to sin again.

Chapter III

The Cooper Field

When Miss Hite was off duty, it fell to a groom to give me a riding lesson, and to Alice Fortune to watch me. She liked the chance to get out of the house and away from the Madam's demanding scrutiny for a while.

I didn't know why, but when we went for a walk Alice always seemed to avoid the barns. It could have been as simple as not being able to chase me up the ladder to the hayloft. Or maybe it was the grooms who tended to be coarse when the family was not in earshot.

But she did like to go to the Cooper field, a small isolated field in a pine clearing well past the barns, pigpens, apple orchard, and finally up a logging road past Dead Horse Hollow where all the dead farm animals were buried. There was a rise in the middle of the field, and on the crest, the scant remains of a fallen-down log cabin. The old logs were mostly rotted away, but the stones from the chimney and foundation were strewn about, some half buried, some on top of each other.

It was a fabulous place to play. While Alice sat on a stone, I marched my army around, under and through the rocks and

*Uncle Jack "riding"
Nootsie the
alcoholic donkey.*

*Grooms
clowning
with
Nootsie.*

logs. I flew my planes, made hangars and revetments for them, and worked on the little pebble town that grew next to the airport. Alice couldn't help with the construction because she was in her uniform, and it had to stay starchy clean even on a long walk. But we kept up a steady patter about what was going on in Coopertown, made up names for the neighbors, and laughed when someone's roof fell off.

When I was with Alice we almost always went up to the Cooper field. It just seemed to happen that way. It never entered my head to wonder why she seemed to enjoy the long walk or the time I spent playing in the little ruin. But close to four decades later, quite by accident, I found out the answer.

After Grandmother died in 1977, Alice retired to West Warm Springs, a little community up behind Webb's store formerly known as "Shakerag."[10] I visited her often and tried to get her to talk about the family, and how she and the other servants coped with the intense demands, criticism, and covert racism they experienced on a daily basis. She told me lots of things about my uncles and their girl friends, about some of the family friends I barely remembered, and stories about the ways everyone maneuvered around the Madam. She was happy to recall the time my father got Nootsie, the donkey, drunk and turned him loose at my grandmother's lawn party. And she described the horrific time my uncle shot his finger off with a starter's cannon.

She talked about her life and the lives and stories of other servants, many of whom had come and gone before my time. But when it came to anything too personal about the family, especially if it involved implied criticism, Alice was cagey—even evasive. She always maintained that no one *really* meant any harm, prejudice was universal, not limited to our family, and one simply learned to deal with it. It could have been worse, and besides, there were plenty of good times.

She told the story of my grandmother wanting to fire Frank Brown, an African-American groom, because he named one of his newborn twin sons "Malcolm" after Uncle Malcolm. It caused quite a row, but Grandfather stopped her. And she did acknowledge how hard it was to serve dinner when a full-blast family fight was going on. But that's as far as she would go. I had to push hard for the nitty-gritty behind-the-scenes stuff I wanted to hear, especially about what she and the other servants talked about when the family wasn't around.

We always met in her living room. Alice sat under an oval-framed picture of her father, Charles Bolden, taken about 1900. He

Alice Fortune's maternal grandmother, Annie Crawford Lindsay Morris was born into slavery on Fort Dinwiddie in 1832. When she was a child, her mother and sisters were sold to a slave owner in South Carolina. She never saw them again. She died in 1917 at the age of 85. (Photograph courtesy of Ms. Perlista Henry).

Freed slave Annie Morris. The picture above was taken about 1902.
The large pile of sawdust in the background may have come from the cooperage, and
suggests the cabin may have been in the Cooper field.
(Photograph courtesy of Ms. Perlista Henry).

drove a carriage for the Homestead, and was dressed in full livery for his portrait. His parents were slaves, as was Alice's maternal grandmother, but her maternal grandfather, Randall Cooper Morris, was a mulatto born a free man because his mother was white. Alice's grandmother was born in 1832 on Fort Dinwidddie.

When Alice's grandmother, Annie Crawford Lindsay Morris, was freed, she and her husband were given a cabin near the fort. Alice was born there in 1899.

It was the cabin in the Cooper field.

After I got past the shock, I asked Alice if she remembered the many hours we spent in the old ruin. She did, and said she always loved to go there and recall the brief but happy time she enjoyed at

Cooper's cabin, as she called it. It "mostly" burned down when she was quite young, and the family moved to Shakerag.

The Cooper field is an isolated, almost inaccessible place today, lost in underbrush, a long hike from the nearest road. But in the 18th and 19th centuries the main road from Warm Springs to Fort Dinwiddie went right through the Cooper field. Alice's grandfather, Randall Cooper, was in fact a cooper, and there was a cooperage along the road, thus the double meaning in the name of the field. There were several other cabins in the immediate vicinity, but no trace of them remains today.

Before emancipation the cabin was probably a simple one-room structure with a large stone fireplace, dirt floor and a sleeping loft. There were at least six to eight slave families living on Dinwiddie at the end of the Civil War. Freedom, however, did not mean that everyone scattered to take advantage of the end of bondage. Far from it. Just because slaves were freed did not give them property, marketable skills, living wages or even the right to move about freely. There were laws that restricted the movement of blacks and dictated how long they could live in certain communities.

The former slaves on Dinwiddie were given the right to live in their cabins, certainly good news, but it also meant being dependent on either the Homestead or landowners for work at take-it-or-leave-it wages. As the 19th century played out, blacks slowly began moving away from plantation-dependence. They became independent blacksmiths, farriers, well diggers, builders, loggers, merchants—and homeowners. And they moved in increasing numbers into the black community of Shakerag.

By the time Alice was born in 1899, the one-room cabin had been expanded to two rooms, each with its own loft. In 1900 there were fourteen to seventeen members of Alice's family living in the Cooper field, along with at least two unrelated former slaves. No one knows for sure who lived where, but it was definitely a crowded place. Most were likely still working on Dinwiddie or in the failing

Alice Fortune's maternal grandfather, Randall Cornelius Morris (1826-1902) was "freeborn" because his mother was white. (Photograph courtesy of Ms. Perlista Henry).

Alice Fortune's father, Charles Bolden (1853-1919) dressed in Homestead livery, taken about 1900. (Photograph courtesy of Ms. Perlista Henry).

cooperage, but some of the others, like Alice's parents, worked at the Homestead.

Life was slowly improving, but amenities were few, and the battle for survival was still harsh and unrelenting. Water was hauled from a spring now just a wet spot at the foot of the hill. The only heat for both rooms in Alice's cabin came from one fireplace. The floor of the room with the fireplace was still dirt as a way to prevent fire. There were woodsheds, a large root cellar, chicken coops, the cooperage, and a barn large enough to hold the Homestead carriage on the nights when Alice's father came home with the coach. No sign of any of it remains today.

Even more haunting—and sad—is the question of where the Cooper field residents are buried. According to Alice, they were all buried in "the slaves graveyard" on an east-facing hill near the field. She pointed it out to her granddaughter, Perlista Henry, when Perlista was a child. I have searched endlessly for it, and when I thought I had found it, I brought in a State archeologist. He wasn't sure. So the final resting place of literally dozens of people remains a mystery.

Alice had no siblings, but Grandfather Cooper Morris was her guardian when her parents were away at work. Alice recalled a large garden, chickens everywhere, a cow and a scary pigpen. Her father commuted to the Homestead on horseback, at least a two-hour ride. When there was work for her seamstress mother, she rode to the Homestead with her husband. When the weather was bad, her parents were sometimes gone for a week at a time. They slept in the Homestead stable when they couldn't get home.

I asked Alice what Christmas was like for her as a little kid. She said her few Christmases at the cabin were among her favorite memories. Store-bought toys were out of the question, and Santa Claus was unknown in those days. Alice's mother saved rags, and throughout the year she wove and sewed them into dolls, and gave Alice a new one every Christmas morning. Alice laughed when I asked her how in that crowded little space her mother managed to conceal her handiwork all year long.

She worked at night when Alice was asleep in the loft, and hid the doll in a trunk no child dared open. Having a small private place in a cramped cabin was a holdover from slavery days. Slaves dug holes in the dirt floor, covering the opening (or "keep") with a flat rock to protect a few precious trinkets or coins. Each keep was sacred; a small hole in the ground, the only way a slave could ever imagine either owning something or having any personal space.

Christmas also meant another rare delight: candy and cookies. Her mother made horehound candy from the wild mint that was—still is—everywhere. But it tasted a lot like the bitter mint tea her mother made as a remedy for all ailments. To Alice, the *real* treat was ginger cookies.

Ginger was expensive and hard to get, a true luxury item. But every Christmas her father brought a precious supply from the Homestead kitchen. About a week before Christmas her mother would say it's time to get the ginger rock ready. A heavy, flat-topped stone was rolled into the fireplace, and hot coals heaped around it twenty-four hours a day until Christmas. Her mother warned that if the rock wasn't hot enough, there wouldn't be any ginger cookies.

On Christmas morning the doll was given, then—weather permitting—the family walked four miles to church in Shakerag. After a long service, social hour and dinner, they returned home for ginger cookies. Alice's mother made the batter, and her father prepared the rock by rubbing it with a piece of fat. The cookies were made one at a time. When the cookie got brown on the edges and stopped bubbling, the edge was lifted and it was peeled off the rock. They rotated around the family until the last drop of batter was gone.

"My goodness! They were good," Alice said in her wonderful giggle-laugh.

When the cabin burned and the family moved to Shakerag, they had a larger cabin with a bigger loft, windows, and a wood stove. Alice could go to school, church was only yards away, and Alice's father came home almost every night. Clearly, life was better away from the isolation of the Cooper field.

But Christmas was never quite the same. Of all her many Christmases, Alice's favorites were at Cooper's cabin with her family sitting in front of the fire making ginger cookies.

I understand exactly what she meant. And I envied her.

Chapter IV

Not You, Not Here

What shall I tell my children who are black
Of what it means to be a captive in this dark skin?
What shall I tell my dear one, fruit of my womb,
Of how beautiful they are when everywhere they turn
They are faced with abhorrence of everything that is black.
The night is black and so is the bogeyman.
Villains are black with black hearts.
A black cow gives no milk. A black hen lays no eggs.
Bad news comes bordered in black, mourning clothes are black.
Storm clouds, black, black is evil
And evil is black and devil's food is black...

What shall I tell my dear ones raised in a white world?
A place where white has been made to represent
All that is good and pure and fine and decent,
Where clouds are white and dolls, and heaven
Surely is a white, white place with angels
Robed in white, and cotton candy and ice cream
And milk and ruffled Sunday dresses

And dream houses and long sleek Cadillacs
And Angel's food is white...all, all...white.

What can I do to give him strength
That he might come through life's adversities
As a whole human being unwrapped and human in a
World of biased laws and inhuman practices, that he might
Survive. And survive he must! For who knows?
Perhaps this black child here bears the genius
To discover the cure for...cancer
Or to chart the course for exploration of the universe.
So, he must survive for the good of all humanity;

He must and will survive.
I have drunk deeply of late from the fountain
Of my black culture, sat at the knee of and learned
From Mother Africa, discovered the truth of my heritage.
The truth so often obscured and omitted.
And I find I have much to say to my black children.
I will lift up their heads in proud blackness
With the story of their fathers and father's Fathers.

For it is the truth that will make us free![11]

The glimpses that Alice and other members of the black community gave me will always be just that: a peek, a hint of the forces operating in their lives. No matter how many facts or individual histories I might uncover, it is impossible for a white son of privilege to write about the black experience in anything approaching a truly insightful way. I didn't live a black life, I only intersected it at times.

Even so, those brief encounters were visceral moments for me, not easily lost even with the passage of time. Many are pleasant—even amusing—to recall, but the majority are uncomfortable, their impact faded but not lost. I am now closing in on my 70's, retired from a medical career and free to go fishing or idle away happy hours in my work shop. Yet in reverie I am drawn back to the past, to specific moments whose images I simply can't shake. The analyst in me wants to externalize and dissect them, because as Margaret Burroughs says, it's "the truth of my heritage...so often obscured..."

When I was around three, just before WWII began for us, I remember being in the little paper mill town of Covington with Alice. About an hour from Warm Springs, it was the nearest town to shop for food and other basics. Trips were always as short as possible because of the nauseating stench of the paper mill. I remember that particular trip because of one brief but terrifying incident.

Alice and I were walking down the main street, a four or five block stretch, courthouse in the middle flanked by a mix of lawyer's offices and small shops. One block over was the only well-provisioned grocery store in the area. Alice was holding my hand and I was likely—as Mother used to complain—"jabbering." It was time for lunch and we turned into a small sandwich shop. It was long and narrow, a blank wall on the left, counter with a dozen or so stools on the right, and a cash register at the end of the counter next to the front door. The instant we walked in the man behind the cash register raised his fist, exploded and yelled—almost screamed—at Alice.

"Get out of here, nigger!!!"

Without saying a word Alice rushed me back to the street. I burst out crying.

"Alice! Why is that man so angry?"

"Don't worry, it's not you," she said as we hurried away. And that's where the memory ends. Alice calmed me, but at the time the outburst made no sense to me. I know that because I've never let go of the image of the angry man I thought was going to attack us. Nor do I forget that Alice's attention was on soothing me, not at all showing any outward concern about her own feelings.

But I can easily guess what she felt, and imagine what she said to the other black employees and members of her family when she was safely home, out of earshot of those who tolerated and encouraged not only the angry sandwich man, but the entire system of segregation. Today, we are concerned about residual racism, but only fifty years ago segregation was the law, and in the South ruled the lives of non-whites.

Taking voting, for example.

As fundamental as the right to vote seems today, in the South following the Civil War Jim Crow laws kept all but a tiny handful of African Americans away from the ballot box. Voting wasn't outright prohibited; instead, disenfranchisement was almost guaranteed by the twin obstacles of the poll tax and literacy test. In Virginia, when I went to register in 1959 at the age of twenty-one, the poll tax was $1.50, a considerable sum for impoverished persons who didn't think their investment in democracy would count anyway.[12]

I walked into the Registrar's Office in Warm Springs and proudly declared I was there to register to vote. The clerk looked horrified, and even though there was no one else in the room with us, she put her index finger to her lips, shrugged her shoulders tightly, and made a "shhhh" sound. She opened the little half door in the counter and led me to a back office, carefully closing the door behind us.

Still whispering, she told me to sit down at her desk. She then opened a large safe, retrieved a one-page document, and placed it on the desk next to a blank sheet of paper.

"Copy it exactly," she said, "Then sign it." The page contained a single long paragraph stating in highly convoluted terms that I the petitioner, having achieved his majority, request the State of

Virginia to blah, blah and uphold the laws blah, blah, attested this day, and signed. The clerk notarized it, and put both pieces of paper back in the safe. I had just passed the literacy test and was now registered to vote.

A black petitioner would have been told to write down his or her request to be registered, then told later that whatever was written had failed to meet the established standards for literacy. Sorry, you can't vote. That was Virginia's system. Had the same person applied in Alabama, a written ten-question test had to be passed, again with the same deadly accuracy as demanded in Virginia. The questions would have challenged any civics teacher. Take Question #6, for example: If a State is a party to a case, the Constitution provides that the original jurisdiction shall be in what court? Guess who got to take this as an open answer sheet exam?

When I talked to Alice about voting she said that for the citizens of Shakerag and Switchback registration wasn't even on the radar screen. Everyone in the black community knew how the literacy test scam worked and they refused to humiliate themselves at the courthouse. Their focus, especially after the Depression hit, was to stay employed and support their families. There was general agreement that most (but certainly not all) of the wealthy employers were fundamentally "prejudiced," but it was just something one had to live with.

It was also true that many families were caring employers, fair and honest people who were immune to racial bias. But even in more fair-minded households, or modest white homes with no servants at all, there was still a divide between those who had, or enjoyed the opportunity to have, and those who were shut out entirely.

It would be a mistake, however, to think that racism was universal, or that in a family like ours where racism was strong, that everyone in the family felt the same way. My two younger uncles, Jack and Malcolm, didn't have a shred of it. It would be equally wrong to assume that all prejudice was directed toward African Americans. My grandmother never used racist language in reference to African Americans; to her, poor and middle class whites were "bumpkins" or "hillbillies." In other parts of the elitist white community the term was "trash."

Take the story of Mary Johnson, for example.

In 1899 Mary Johnson wrote a best-selling novel: *To Have and To Hold*. She made a great deal of money from the book, came to Bath County and built a huge home on top of a hill overlooking Warm Springs. She lived there with her sister Eloise, entertained her fans, and struggled in vain to write a great follow-up hit novel. After she died in the mid-1930's, Eloise turned the place into an inn. Servants were instructed not to allow tradesmen or undesirables through the front door; of course, that was understood to include all blacks. One day a game warden, chasing a pack of dogs that had been killing sheep, came to the front door asking if anyone had seen the dogs. Eloise exploded over the intrusion of what she called "trash," and refused to speak to the warden until he went around to the back door and was admitted to the kitchen.

It would be equally wrong to think that even in the days of segregation racism was always the in-your-face variety. True, I often heard whites of every stripe use the word "nigger," often within earshot of blacks. But most people held their tongue in public. You could still see contempt in their faces, or feel it in their body language, but it was rare to hear blatantly racist remarks out loud.

One older member of the African American community who knew my grandfather quite well was surprised to hear me say he was a racist.

"I never heard him say anything prejudiced," he said. Obviously, outside of the home he hid his feelings well; after all, he was a showman, a man who was always aware of his audience.

Although I felt close to Alice literally from my earliest recollections, I hadn't the tiniest clue about her personal life. It wasn't until my grandmother died and we started talking that I began to appreciate her struggle to overcome the smothering effect of life in our family and the white community in general. I say in the family, because my grandparents (and all employers of the day, according to Alice) understood the role of a servant to be one of adherence to the very fabric of the family. They had to pretend a kind of loyalty that added to the family's sense of security and importance. Perhaps I'm going out on a limb with this, but it seems to me to have been a watered-down extension of slavery. My grandfather made no bones about his resentment of the idea of giving legal or social status to blacks, Jews, the Irish, or anyone else he deemed inferior. It was an attitude built into a substantial portion of our society at the time.

I tried to imagine my grandfather's reaction had he been able to read the last paragraph. First of all, he would have blistered me for airing the family's business in public. When he got over that hurdle, he would have said he was a realist, not a racist. My guess is he would have said (as Alice, Martha and others did) that good jobs were hard to find, and that life in our family was a whole lot better than toiling in the Homestead laundry. He would have said that his attitudes were no different from the vast majority of whites in the south (another point of agreement), and the slavery idea was utter rubbish. I am dead certain he would have defended the paternalistic notion that most "Negroes" are little more than children who need a lot of support and direction to get by.

He would also have asked if I am so high-and-mighty troubled by past manifestations of prejudice, how come I accepted the voting registration literacy test without the slightest complaint? He would have argued you can't go back in time, ask people to have been clairvoyant, and sanctimoniously beat them up with 20-th century standards. When he was born, slavery had only been gone for thirteen years, and everyone used the word "nigger." It's the way it was at the time.

I would have to concede his point about registration, I didn't protest. But on the subject of the word "nigger" I would respond that even as a kid I knew it was a powerful and ugly word, and hearing it out loud made me and lot of others cringe. And I do think one can go back in time—carefully, of course—and say that simply because racism was a well subscribed regional attitude doesn't make it any less wrong. And what I am talking about here isn't some set of quiet assumptions, it's overt, aggressive racism. I heard Grandfather tell his butler, Carey Underwood, he was a "good nigger." He said it right to his face, and it made me uncomfortable enough to remember it sixty years later.

Another recollection I have is my father's enthusiastic description of the one of his and Grandfather's favorite entertainments, the Battle Royal. Sold as "sport," the Battle Royal

Grandfather's butler, Carey Underwood.

was popular in the twenties and thirties, especially in the early part of the Depression when times were desperate and people were literally eating crow. The Battle Royal was a chance to make some big money, even if you did have to risk serious injury to get it.

The "battle" took place in a Covington theater. A prize-fighting ring was set up on the stage and 10-15 black "fighters" were put in the ring. There were different battles for different age groups starting with kids and progressing to young adults. At the bell everyone started punching, and the fighting went on until there was only one person left standing.

We have a winner! He collected the purse and the next group stepped up. The rationalization for the Battle Royal was the fact someone walked (or hobbled) off with a fat cash prize, enough to feed a family for quite a while. Again, the argument was that no real harm was done, someone benefited and to the extent it was another form of racism, well, so what? That's the way it was at the time, and everybody—including blacks—knew and accepted it.

But speaking to Alice's granddaughter, Perlista Henry, one hears a vastly different story. On the surface, yes, there was acceptance at the time that 'for now' that was the way it had to be, and—yes—it wasn't all bad. African Americans in Bath (and everywhere else) quietly and unobtrusively did what they had to do not only to survive, but continue to evolve their own culture—in spite of all the obstacles surrounding society presented. Based on a shared history and a strong sense of spirituality, a socially cohesive community developed and thrived.

Slow and steady wins the race. Today, most of the children of area black families are college educated and have moved away to careers in distant places. Those who remain seem to this outsider to be fully part of the community at large, though I'm sure there are lingering pockets of racism on one side and despair on the other.

Remember Malcolm Brown, the boy whose father my grandmother wanted to fire for naming his child after her son? He grew up to become a successful artist. His twin brother, Milton, is also an artist, and a career officer in the United States Air Force. The twins are standing in the front row, right side, in the "Our Employees" picture.

But I'm certain there is a lot of residual resentment over the obvious fact it has taken so long for real progress to have been made. More than a hundred years have gone by since Alice was born in the old slave cabin, and fifty since segregation was officially declared dead. That's a long time to do the obvious.

But in the meantime, regardless of the reality beyond, the black community is and has always been a vibrant place. Then as now, virtually every family expresses pride in its ancestors, and a keen awareness of what they endured as well as what still must change. To be sure, there is immense lingering anger over slavery and the endless pain of segregation, but at the same time—and not mutually exclusive—there is pride in what was "overcome." That is why that word means so much in the anthem of change. When I talk to some of the older members of the community, there is nostalgia over what it meant to be the children and grandchildren of slaves, and members of the black community.

It wasn't all work and no play, either.

Take the Airship, for instance. On a narrow rutted road behind the Homestead stable in the little town of Hot Springs a tall four-story house with porches all around stood with its back against a vertical cliff. It was a combination boarding house, restaurant, barber shop and general meeting place for black people, most employed by the hotel. Female employees lived on the second floor, men on the two floors above. The top floor was called the "Ape Yard," not as a racist slur, but because it was literally at treetop level. The barbershop and restaurant were on the first floor, areas where a lot of socializing took place.

No one seems to know just how the Airship got its name. Maybe it was the sheer height of the building and the improbability of it being able to stand flat and unanchored against the cliff. Or maybe it was because of the people who jumped off the roof—took to the air, so to speak—on a regular basis.

Members of the volunteer fire department used the Airship in the 1920's and 1930's to hone their fire fighting skills. A crowd always gathered on practice day to watch the men scale up the outside of the building and onto the roof wearing heavy coats, rubber boots and dragging a long, heavy hose. The real excitement, though, was watching someone jump off the roof into the rescue net. The only known casualty was Floyd Carpenter who missed the net and broke his hip. It's a wonder no one was killed.

The Airship's restaurant was called the Hot Springs Grill or the Green Onion, depending on whom you ask. After hours it was known as the "Teapot" because beer was served in teapots, not glasses, bottles or cans. There was no disagreement about the food, though. The people who cooked at the Airship were all Homestead trained, and the food was excellent.

Things weren't always tranquil at the Airship. The white community regarded it as something of a wild place, and while it certainly had its moments, it was an excellent alternative to other hotel housing, and an accessible and popular place to socialize. But it is true that whites were not generally welcome. A friend told me a story about a close call he had while making a delivery of soft drinks. The cooler was on the third floor porch, and while he was filling it, a man came out of his room and, thinking he was a robber, pulled out a knife. My friend jumped off the porch three stories to the ground, hobbled to his truck, drove off, and never went back.

Not far from the Airship, just across the main street and the railroad tracks, there was another popular black hangout, the Tea Room (not to be confused with the Teapot) where the food was just as good as it was at the Airship. But there was an added twist at the Tearoom: a second floor dining room and dance hall catering to the more daring, late-night Homestead crowd. Food and spirits were served upstairs well into the night, way past the time the more sedate Homestead dining room closed. And the music was different, too. While the Homestead orchestra played lullaby classics in the Crystal Room, there was jazz, swing and jitterbug at the Tea Room played by local, mostly black musicians.

Next door to the Tea Room was Smith's Chapel, a small church attached to the end of the large dormitory the Homestead maintained for most of its staff, including married employees. If you wanted to hear great gospel music, Smith's Chapel was the place to go. Touring gospel groups made the rounds of area black churches, but when they hit the Chapel the music went from a service to a concert. Big-name touring groups like Wings over Jordan, The Swinston Brothers, and The Sunset Travelers were regulars.

There were two other popular black gathering places, both hardly known in the white community. Just behind Webb's store on the edge of Shakerag was Hugh Daley's Hall, a restaurant, dance hall, boarding house, and place where both local and touring black bands played. I was surprised to learn that there were two other smaller restaurants in Shakerag. They all survived in large part because the black waiters and staff from the Homestead regularly socialized there.

Just below Hot Springs in the woods only a hundred yards or so from the waiter's dormitory was an old house that had fallen on hard times. For a while it was a recreation hall, but it evolved into something of a nightclub. The floors were crooked, the doors didn't quite close, and some of the windows were boarded up. But it had running water and electricity, and right into the early 1950's there was a dance there almost every Saturday night. It was known in the black community as "The Rec," but whites generally understood it to be "The Wreck." Just depends on where you stand.

One of the bands that played there regularly was the Rhythm Makers, an R&B band from near-by Lexington. They started in Philadelphia, recorded several albums, and were popular on the

Queen Esther Pullins and Red Williams play for a white audience, probably at Grandfather's picnic grounds on the Jackson River in 1935. My father is in the middle wearing a straw boater. (Photograph courtesy of Mrs. Diana Richmond).

East Coast from Boston to Atlanta, especially in black clubs and on college campuses. Their singer was a remarkable man named Lewis Watts born with no arms and said to have a voice like Billy Eckstine. In spite of his handicap, Watts graduated from college, was a champion horse shoe player (he threw with his feet), slow-pitch softball pitcher (feet again: he put the ball on the ground, planted his toes in the dirt behind the ball and flick-kicked it toward the batter), and wizard pool shooter (he used a bridge and held the cue stick against his neck with his chin). He was also an artist (he held the paintbrush in his teeth), and toward the end of his career taught music in New York City. Both Jet and Life Magazines wrote feature articles about the amazing musician with no arms.

There was music everywhere in the black community. It was in the churches, at the Chapel, in the Homestead's dormitory, at the Airship, at the Rec, upstairs at the Tea Room, at picnics, family reunions, and in people's homes. There were bands, choirs and individual performers, some of who performed regularly and for good money outside of the community.

One of the most talented performers was a piano player named Red Williams, not surprisingly because he had light hair and a reddish complexion. He often teamed up with another musician, a guitar player named James "Queen Esther" Pullins (he got his nickname from an old jazz performer). Queen Esther learned guitar from his mother who was a great musician herself. She played guitar and harp (harmonica), and lived to be over 100.

These men could play anything. Unlike my grandfather's fabled play-by-ear story, Red really could play anything he heard just once. He and my grandfather knew each other, and Red was one of a very small number of black musicians invited to play for Grandfather's "fling-dings" at his riverside picnic grounds. The man in the center of the picture of Red Williams and Queen Esther is my father, and that makes it likely the picture was taken at the picnic grounds.

Todd Jones (1897-1956), Alice Fortune's first husband,
WWI veteran and accomplished musician.
This 1921 photograph shows him playing a Dyer harp guitar by Larson Brothers.
(Photograph courtesy of Ms. Perlista Henry).

Sometimes the music didn't quite work, though. Take Frances Poole's Huskies, for example. She called herself "Frances Poole of India" (her tombstone reads "The Pooles of India"), claiming she came from India and had fortune-telling powers. She was 6'6" tall, wore bib overalls most of the time, and was called Highpockets behind her back. She was a stern woman who lived alone and raised Siberian Huskies. Everyone was careful around Highpockets, especially local white politicians whom she frequently (though not always successfully) challenged over the persistent denial of water, sanitation and trash services in her community.

Among her claims was that she had trained her dogs to sing gospel music, and one day she brought her canine choir to church to perform. But the dogs apparently weren't up to singing that day. They howled and barked a bit, but that was about it. Highpockets withdrew in a huff.

Another major issue in the African American community was education; or more accurately, the lack of it. The rules of slavery said blacks were not to be taught to read and write. Even music was banned by many white slave owners. After emancipation the opportunity to receive an education came slowly. Well into the 20th century there were only two schools available to black youngsters—one on each side of the county—and no high school at all until 1933!

Alice and her contemporaries attended the Jones school in Shakerag until it closed in the early 1930's. Ironically, the school was built on land donated by Alice's great-grandfather, William Jones, a successful blacksmith in the little community west of Warm Springs.

When the Jones school was closed, all of the students changed to the Union Hurst School in Switchback about ten miles away. In spite of distance and the crushing limitations of the Depression, families did everything they could to get their kids to the new school. Union Hurst was a house with a large cafeteria on the ground floor, and three rooms above. Grades 1-4 were in one room, 5-7 in another, and 8-12 in the third. There was a wood-burning stove in every room, but no running water—thus no indoor plumbing. Before lunch every student had to take one teaspoon full of cod liver oil. No matter what was served, it all tasted like fish.

Union Hurst graduated the first black high school student in 1937. She was also the only member of her class! Now in her eighties, Clara Henry Black lives near the abandoned school.

In the 1940's, high school students were shifted from Union Hurst to the Watson School in Covington, a very long commute even by today's standards. Even though the landmark Brown vs. Board of Education ruling came in 1954, it wasn't until 1959 that the first black students entered a mainstream Virginia high school.

A birthday party at Union Hurst, hopefully without a dose of cod liver oil first.
(Photograph courtesy of Mr. Roger Anderson).

In 1958 the state closed 9 schools in 4 counties to avoid integration, and it was 1967 before total integration was achieved.

Union Hurst survives, an abandoned shell on the hill above the road, a symbol of what was endured and overcome. There is talk of restoring the old building, a way to remember history that is so easily and conveniently forgotten.

Back in Warm Springs, the Confederate War Memorial stands large and bold on the lawn in front of the County Courthouse, its proud granite soldier standing guard over the words **LEST WE FORGET.**

Alice's life was its own monument, remembered without words carved in stone. In spite of her long workdays and constant moves back and forth from New Jersey with my grandparents, Alice raised three children. Alice and her daughter Madeline died three days apart, and were mourned in the same ceremony at the Mount Pisgah Church (founded in 1876 by Alice's grandparents). At the time of her death, Alice was its oldest member. Mother Alice, as she was known, left behind 11 great-grandchildren, 24 great-great grandchildren, and 6 great-great-great grandchildren.

Chapter V

Taming of the Shrews

About the same time I was talking with Alice, quite by accident I ran into another woman who had worked for Grandmother. I was doing a medical consultation at a small nursing home in nearby Clifton Forge when I ran into Martha, my grandmother's cook for several decades. Like Alice, I remember her as a friendly, warm woman, full of good humor, and somehow always well above the Madam's peckishness.

She was in her late eighties, sharp as a tack but physically fragile. She had a walker but it gathered dust in the corner; instead, she used a cane and the wall for support, hiding any discomfort behind a steady, cheerful patter. She lived in a bedroom with three other residents. The home was Spartan at best, a place that accepted generally poor folks on Medicaid, and used its limited resources as best it could to give its residents some modicum of privacy and comfort. From the outside, it was a slightly run down brick rancher with a birdbath on each side of the sidewalk, and some year-round Christmas lights over the door. Except for the name on the mailbox, you couldn't tell it was a nursing home, the last stop for its dozen or so residents.

Inside, it was stuffy hot, and the unmistakable smell of fading lives hung in the air displaced only at meal time when everyone gathered in the dining room to eat whatever came out of large tin cans. But it was also tidy, the TV worked, and the nurse and the aide who ran the place were endlessly cheerful and caring.

I've seen a lot of such places over the years. Supported only by miserly Medicaid payments sometimes supplemented by a resident's Social Security, they struggle to offer even the most basic services. Typically, the facility gets the resident's entire monthly income, leaving only five or ten dollars a month to buy extras like toothpaste and cigarettes. Even for the lucky ones who have some degree of family support, it's a terribly constricted, isolated, bare-bones existence. And if there is no family support, the individual is utterly alone, trapped by age, infirmity and poverty.

Martha's husband was for many years the headwaiter at the Homestead Casino, an open-air restaurant next to the tennis

The Homestead waiters' tray race on the lawn of the Casino.
(Photograph courtesy of Mr. Roger Anderson).

courts between the hotel and first tee of the golf course.[13] He was a formidable man, tall and somewhat stern looking. He ran the dining room with an iron fist, remembered every guest by name, and always seemed calm and unflappable no matter how impatient or demanding guests might be. I was slightly afraid of him as a kid, not so much because of his stature or anything he ever said to me, but because of the way my parents reacted to him. They were downright respectful, and never (that I recall) called him anything but his name—Farrington.

One of the most humiliating rituals I saw as a kid was the Homestead waiters' tray race. All of the waiters—without exception—were African Americans, and because Farrington was a headwaiter, he had to run the tray race. Waiters dressed in formal green and white uniforms with polished brass buttons lined up with huge loaded trays balanced on their heads.

All the waiters had numbers, and a large board of the sort you would see at a horse track or golf tournament was set up to keep track of the racers. White lanes were drawn on the grass, and guests bet on their favorites. At the signal, the waiters 'raced' across the lawn, everyone cheering wildly for his or her favorite. When the race was over, trophies were awarded and bets paid off.

I found the following description of the "Homestead Waiters Tray Race" in an old scrapbook, dated by hand "1954." The magazine from which it came was not identified.

In the earliest days of The Homestead Hotel colored waiters were drawn from plantation hands. It was traditional for these negroes to carry burdens on their heads, and as Homestead waiters it seemed natural to carry their trays in that manner...In the Spring and again in the Fall, a tray race is held on the Casino lawn. The October race had fifteen entries and was run in three preliminary heats and finals...There was a great cheering of favorite (sic) and some humor whenever a contestant tried to make up lost ground and stumbled, spilling the china with a crash.

I saw a variation of the race called the "Tray Dance" which was held indoors in the Crystal Room. Waiters balanced trays loaded with water glasses, china and lighted candles, or potted plants on their heads. Again the scrapbook:

They go through an elaborate clog dance, keeping the tray balanced on their heads. So far we have never heard of a catastrophe.

A Homestead waiter gets ready for the
Tray Dance in the Crystal Room.
(Photograph courtesy of Mr. Roger Anderson).

After the dance guests threw money on the floor and waiters scurried around picking it up.

But not Farrington. He stood aside or busied himself with the trays, the same serious look on his face. Farrington didn't grovel. I'll bet that's why my parents never had anything negative to say about the man.

The races were discontinued later in the 1950's as everyone became more aware of their essentially racist nature. Recently, I tried to get permission from the Homestead to use one of their photographs of the race. The hotel historian politely declined saying that this is not the image the hotel wants to project. He was not the least defensive about it; rather, it seemed to him an unfortunate historical fragment, something better left behind. I certainly understand his sensitivity. But on the positive side it should be noted the Homestead responded strongly when the issue of racism burst into public awareness in the aftermath of *Brown vs. Board of Education*, well ahead of many other institutions that clung tenaciously to their right to be wrong.

Another aside on the racism issue. The Casino china was deep blue, and in the center of each piece was a picture of a waiter with a tray on his head. One night a crew from the kitchen came down to the Casino and broke every single dish showing the tray picture. Even the black employees were startled.

"I understand why they wanted to destroy them, but those dishes were beautiful. I wish I had one of them today," I was told by a woman who worked with Farrington, and gave the Homestead 44 years of service.

When I met Martha again, Farrington had been dead for at least ten years. She couldn't keep up with the physical demands of her house in Hot Springs, so she reluctantly moved to the nursing facility. Her life was reduced to a bed, a bureau and a never-off color TV in the combination recreation/dining room.

We chatted about the past. Memories came easily, and so did the laughs. There was nothing funny to say about the present so we stuck to stories about the drunken mule at the garden party, and Malcolm's many girl friends. Over time, I edged back to the questions that always haunted me: what was it really like dealing with my family day to day? How did you cope? Did you ever think Farrington would storm in, scream "That's enough!" and take you out of there?

But Martha was every bit as cagey as Alice. I heard the same blandishments: prejudice was universal and no worse in your house than anywhere else, life was tougher in other parts of the south, we were too lucky to be working to worry about our employer's attitudes toward race. And so on.

Then I got lucky. On what was literally my last visit with Martha she gave in a little. Just a glimpse, mind you, but a telling peek it was.

It all had to do with the servant's dining room. Along with servant's living quarters, each house had a dining room behind the kitchen where the servants ate and socialized. Martha explained that sometimes, when the chores were all finished and the family had retired, they would all gather in their dining room, close the door, and open a bottle of wine.

"Then we put on our play. We all had our parts."

"Your play?" I puzzled. "What was your play?"

"Well," she said with a big smile, "It was called **The Hirsh Family.** And it was *fun!*" She laughed at the memory.

Lord! What I wouldn't give to have been a fly on the wall of the servant's quarters. But in a way, this was better. Thanks, Martha, you've explained it perfectly.

Chapter VI

Heroes

Everyone needs a hero, but they're mighty hard to find. While our lives may be full of people we admire and look up to, it's rare for one to become an enduring, personal hero. Heroes don't come and go, or last for a summer or two. They show up early, get our attention, and over time give us something valuable we would have otherwise missed. Heroes make a profound difference in our life course; even after they're dead, we continue to answer to them.

And I'm not talking about long-distance heroes or idols. History, both contemporary and remote, is full of galvanic figures. We all have our favorites, and sometimes we try to mimic or emulate the heroic distillate. But that's a conscious process, an attempt to shape personality or manipulate values based on what we see as a good example. It's an add-on, doesn't change who we are in any profound or lasting sense, and lapses the minute we forget our lines.

The hero I'm talking about is a compass-turner who shows up out of pure dumb luck, and becomes part of who we are without design or intention. It just happens.

That lets out religious figures. Theirs is a deliberate teaching, instruction role, designed to form one around their sense of the cosmos. Heroes don't teach or even try to be anything beyond themselves. A hero simply *is*. By being who they are, they have an effect on you alone. It's personal. Your hero may not appeal to anyone else. It doesn't matter a bit.

The best of parents can be heroic, but they can't be heroes. They're parents, and by doing the best they can, they give us the tools we need for success in both a moral and material sense. Being a firm, loving parent who guides with a clear example of personal and community responsibility puts you in the Parents Hall of Fame. But it doesn't make you a hero. The reverse is also true: a hero isn't a parent, and should not be compared to one. Their roles are entirely different.

A hero comes from outside the immediate family group. It can be an uncle, an aunt, a cousin, a family friend, a clerk at the feed store, an employee. It doesn't matter, as long the relationship has a clear, positive, never-fade effect on you. The ultimate criterion is: a hero makes your life different.

My first hero was Uncle Gene Folks. He wasn't a real uncle, you know the kind I mean: the person so close and loved by your family that being "Mister Folks" wouldn't do. "Uncle Gene;" ah!, that's more like it.

Gene was born in a remote part of Bath County in 1919. He weighed 13 pounds at birth, apparently a state record. "It stood for years," he told me, "The only record I ever held." His father, a merchant and at one time the county sheriff, was sixty when Gene was born. His mother was a teacher, and while her husband was sheriff she kept order in the jail, fed the county prisoners, and made sure they got to court on time.

Sheriff Folks tolerated a little moonshining, just enough for local consumption, but he did go after any larger operations, a dangerous undertaking as we will see a little later. Otherwise, he saw his job as "keepin' the lid on," jailing drunks before they killed someone, and not letting the gambling at the Homestead spill over into the community.

Gene was a smart, can-do country boy equally at home hunting and fishing in the back woods, teaching swimming at the Homestead, or working in his parent's dry goods store. He and his brother, Alfred, and Sam Snead and his brother Pete, were the stars of the Valley High football teams in the early 1930's. In 1936 Gene and Pete Snead formed a band called the Dipsie Doodles; Sam Snead was a trumpet player, but he preferred to play in the private gambling clubs at the Greenbriar in near-by White Sulfur Springs, West Virginia.

Gene says his band was the first integrated band the county had ever seen. He played guitar and saxophone (Conn B flat sax, a gift from Uncle Jack), Pete Snead played tenor sax, "Frenchman," a cook at the Homestead, played drums, and Red Williams was on piano. They played anywhere they were guaranteed $48.00 for the night, paid in advance. Another requirement was an easy way out in case people got too liquored up and started a brawl.

It's easy today to overlook the importance of Gene's integrated band, but in the mid-1930's it was truly radical. That it happened at all is amazing enough, but the ready acceptance in the community at large was nothing short of astonishing.

Until the Dipsie Doodles came along, music in the county was divided into three separate groups. The first (and least important—included only for the sake of completeness) was the formal music played at the Homestead. Even in the 1950's when Rock and Roll was being played everywhere else, the stiff, formal sounds of the dance orchestra droned on in repetitive, but safe, monotony. Though it was dull, it was indeed beautiful music, and I was surprised to hear a number of older former employees say how much they loved it and considered hearing it a work bonus.

The white people who had grown up on small farms in the hollows used stringed instruments and played true, old-time mountain music. Using banjos borrowed from slaves, fiddles mainly from Scottish tradition, and guitars evolved from lutes and harps, they played jigs, hornpipes, reels, ballads, and square dance tunes brought from Ireland, England and Scotland. They sang Protestant hymns in church; at first, *a capella*, later accompanied by the pump organ. Over time the music was influenced by other genres like ragtime and the blues. By the time the Depression hit, the Carter Family and Jimmy Rogers were selling huge numbers of records of what was widely called "hillbilly" music, a style that evolved in the late thirties into bluegrass and country music.

The banjo had African roots, and came to the south through the West Indies. There, it was a four-stringed instrument called either the "banza" or "banjar." Thomas Jefferson wrote in 1781 that it was the proper instrument of the black slaves, and it remained so until the early 1800's when whites started to play it. The fifth, or drone string, was more widely introduced by Joel Sweeney, a popular white minstrel banjo player who was born in 1810. Both four and five-stringed banjos continued to be played.

After emancipation, blacks dropped the banjo like a hot coal; they associated it with slavery. When the blues and ragtime began, black performers used the piano, mouth harp and guitar. The Martin Company started producing quality guitars in 1833. That instrument was—and remains—popular with everyone, and carried no negative association with slavery.

African American music was a lot more than banzas. Slaves brought songs, chants, unique rhythms and knowledge of other instruments, mostly percussive, from Africa. The lyrics of their songs were often allegorical, seemingly speaking of rotten behavior in their own group, but in reality directed—as all blacks knew—at oppressive slave owners, and later at exploitative landowners, police, and municipal officers. Their music followed a clear path to the blues and jazz.

Banjo player Issac "Ike" Alexander Taylor Smith (1881-1966)
stood 5'4" tall and was known as "the short man with a long name."
He made the neck of his homemade banjo from a discarded railroad tie.
(Photograph courtesy of Mr. and Mrs. Forrest Ford).

But in Bath County the relatively large number of talented black musicians had virtually no opportunity to perform for white audiences—or for money.

The Dipsie Doodles changed that. And it happened when Gene was only 17.

Gene came into our family either through Uncle Malcolm, or perhaps because of his band. It doesn't matter. Grandfather admired his musicianship, recognized his intelligence, and encouraged him to go to college to study engineering. If he did, and wanted to work in his engineering business, he was guaranteed a job. It was a promise Grandfather kept.

Gene and Malcolm were the same age and shared a sense of mischief. An example is their brief but highly successful Homestead Tennis Ploy. Malcolm, a middling player, introduced Gene—a

Whit Bogan (left) and his brother Charlie in Bacova, early 1920's.
(Photograph courtesy of Mrs. Mary Bogan Broce).

natural athlete and already the Homestead swimming instructor—to the game of tennis. In short order Gene developed a devastating serve, and his speed allowed him to cover the court "like a rug," as Malcolm used to say.

Gambling on social games was highly prevalent at the time. Even during the Depression the wealthy continued to come to the Homestead. Some took a "summer cottage," and settled into a three-month holiday of endless golf and tennis with old friends. At night they ate long and well, went to a movie, then danced the night away. The band played at dinner, the orchestra (the band, augmented) played late into the night, and the Arthur Murray dance couple entertained with a dazzling medley of Samba, Rumba and Cha Cha steps. Steps, by the way, you could learn at their studio in the bell tower.

"Because," they explained at the conclusion of every show, "If *your* dancing isn't becoming to *you*, then you should be coming to *us*!"

A little wager always spiced up the endless games of golf or tennis. Enter Malcolm, dressed in proper tennis whites, ready to play. Singles anyone? They played, Malcolm was seen to be a fairly good tennis player, and bets were made. Malcolm would generally come out on the short end, and would then be drawn into a doubles match where the big money was to be found. Malcolm, lacking a partner, said he would get the swimming teacher to play with him, but asked they all be kind to this young and inexperienced country boy who was just learning the game. A great to-do was made over getting Gene some whites; more money was anteed up, and the game began. Gene, of course, was all over the place smacking winners, and possibly with a little help from Malcolm, they handily beat all comers.

The Homestead caught onto the scam and took care of the problem by doing the obvious: they made Gene the assistant tennis pro. End of wagers.

In the late 1930's, Gene went to The University of Chicago and majored in engineering. It was a huge change for him, and a financial risk for his family. As he was finishing college, WWII broke out, and Gene volunteered for the Marine Corps. He trained for six months, was promoted to First Lieutenant, and shipped across the Pacific to Guadalcanal in charge of a mortar platoon. He was wounded twice, returning to battle both times. He summed it all up saying "I spent two years sleeping in the mud and getting shot at all the time."

From the *Bath County Enterprise*, May 24, 1945; first printed in the *New York Herald Tribune*, written by a Marine captain who witnessed it.

The Marine Lieutenant calmly ignored the Jap sniper who was knocking chips from rocks and foliage around him, and in a steady clear voice directed firing until mortar men in his platoon drove the Japs from their positions, enabling two companies to advance.

None of the Marines on Motobu Peninsula who saw the performance of 26 year-old First Lieutenant Gene Folks, of Hot Springs, Virginia, were surprised. Men in his battalion rated the one-time tennis professional man as good as any mortar platoon in the Marine Corps.

"That sniper must have fired at him 15 times. Don't ask me why he wasn't hit."

When Folks called for the last burst, it fell 40 yards from where he stood.

When the war ended in 1945, my three uncles all came home—more or less safely. Father had volunteered, but was rejected because it was thought he had a heart condition. He spent the war as a neighborhood air raid warden. Because we lived near the New Jersey coast, air raids were a constant occurrence. When the siren sounded, we pulled down the black shades and switched on lamps with yellow lights. Father—the man with a heart condition—had to lug a pump fire extinguisher full of water (40-50 pounds) and a bucket of sand (30 pounds) down the long driveway, stand on the curb until the all-clear sounded, then drag it all back.

He was in great shape by the end of the war, lived to his mid-eighties, and died of non-cardiac reasons.

Father's rejection was a major blow to the Madam. Mothers whose sons or daughters were serving in the armed forces showed

"Uncle" Gene Folks in Marine boot camp 1943
shortly before he was shipped out to fight in the Pacific.
(Photograph courtesy of Captain Gene Folks, USMC).

their pride and sacrifice with stars, either displayed in a window, on the front door or worn as a pin—one star for each soldier. The Madam was caught in a competition for stars with a neighbor in Montclair who already had three sons in the Army, and proudly wore a colorful three-star pin. Father's rejection meant the Madam would not be able to trump her neighbor. With sons Allan and Jack already safely in training, her hopes rested on the shoulders of her youngest, Malcolm. Clearly, she couldn't have more stars than her neighbor. But she damn well could have *better* stars, so she went to Van Cleef & Arpels jewelers in New York, and ordered a diamond and sapphire broach.

There was just one little snag: before she could pin on the triumphal broach, Malcolm had to be accepted into the Army. He dutifully went off to Roanoke, had his physical exam, and blood was drawn for the Wasserman test, the standard test for syphilis at the time. He was pronounced fit and ready, and told to report in two weeks. When he arrived home, the Madam was waiting, pin in hand.

Malcolm came in shaking his head and looking grim.

"Well?!" she demanded, "Did you make it?!"

"No," he said in mock sadness, "I flunked my Wasserman test."

"Well," she huffed dismissively, "We'll get you a tutor!"

The Madam got to wear her pin, Jack went to aviation school, and Allan became an artillerist and was shipped to France. Malcolm was sent to Alaska where he claims to have survived the crash of a B-26 in the Aleutian Islands. I say "claims" because others doubt the story's truth. He was a tail gunner and flew patrols in the Aleutians, and I heard him tell the story a number of times. True or not, it was a great tale, and maybe it did happen.

Before the war he was a skeet shooting whiz claiming to have been "East Coast Champion," though that turned out to be an exaggeration. Because of his sense of how to lead a moving target, it was only natural to make him a gunner on a bomber. He was a tail gunner, jammed into a tiny compartment he had to share with the plane's weather-sensing gear, and during endless patrols along the Aleutians answered the pilot's requests for various readings, all of which, Malcolm noted, were always the same.

To make his accommodations more comfortable, he removed some of the weather gear and lined the space with two thin, doubled mattresses. When asked for a reading he simply looked out of the window and gave an answer. Then he went back to his magazine. One day the plane developed engine trouble and was forced to make an emergency landing. On impact, the plane split in half, but thanks to his cushioning, Malcolm survived with nothing more than a nosebleed. Some of the crew were not as fortunate. His arrangement was discovered, he was demoted and spent the rest of the war in California teaching skeet shooting to gunnery students. It could have been worse. He didn't care a bit about the demotion and was happy to be back shooting skeet every day.

Uncle Jack came home unscratched. While in the service he learned to fly, but the war ended before he saw combat.

Uncle Allan came back from France a brevet artillery major. He also brought home his French "war bride" and her 7 year-old daughter, neither of whom spoke a word of English. Alice told me that the Madam exploded and in a burst of fury washed every window in the house, and didn't acknowledge the new bride for the better (or worse) part of a year.

Gene returned after the Japanese surrender in September, 1945. Everyone was glad to see Gene, and like my uncles, he had amazing stories to tell. He moved to New Jersey, went to work for my grandfather, and we all got to see a lot of Gene.

When he drove to his home in Bath he sometimes took me along. It was a long ride and we often spent the night along the way. Gene talked about the war, what makes a good driver, how to deal with vapor lock, and how to outsmart the class bully. He seemed to know something about everything. We drove the Blue Ridge Parkway, hit all the caverns and ate in what my parents called "greasy spoons." We stopped at just about every roadside attraction between New Jersey and Bath County.

My favorite stop was Dr. Childress' Snake and Monkey Farm on old Route 11 in the Shenandoah Valley. Hardly a "farm," it was about the size of a Dairy Queen, and featured dozens of rattlesnakes caught up on the Blue Ridge, and a grumpy chimp with a red ass and hardly any hair. The chimp had some sort of eczema, and only stopped scratching long enough to throw a fist full of peanut shells at anyone who got too close to the cage.

In Bath we stayed at Gene's family place in Burnsville, a remote crossroads with little more than a few houses and a general store/post office. His mother cooked the fish we caught for breakfast, along with some homemade sausage, fresh eggs and apple butter. We had country ham or steaks for dinner, plenty of vegetables from the garden and fresh milk. Simple. And none of the cold celery soup, jellied madrilène, salsify and tongue served up regularly in our house.

During the day we took long walks through the fields, along the river, and up into the woods. I heard about his uncle who got trapped on a shed roof for two days by wolves. And yonder, by that barn, that's where his grandfather killed a bear with an ax. He was splitting wood, his dog barked and when he turned around a bear was standing right behind him.

"Yup, split his head with that ax. Killed him dead as two AM."

We fished a lot. With a little can of Vienna Sausages (pronounced Vi-Enna), a pack of saltines, and a Royal Crown, you were ready for a mile of the Calfpasture River. Along the way, we caught crawfish, hellgrammites and grasshoppers for bait, ducked the occasional irritable ram or bull, and brought home some fat bass.

At night Gene and his mother sang and played whatever was at hand. They knew every hymn in the book all the way through, no matter how many verses there were. Inspired by Gene's easy style of guitar playing, I bought a guitar, he showed me a few chords so I could play along. The old Black Diamond strings cut my fingers and I couldn't strike a clear chord. Doesn't matter, said Gene, keeping time is far more important; the chords will come. That was the beginning of my life-long love affair with the guitar.

Sometimes Gene and his mother just told stories: the prisoner who tried to escape and wound up locking himself in a broom closet; the guy who put a bucket on a rope and left it under the grate behind the jail where confiscated moonshine was dumped; the two escaped convicts who holed up for months in a cave behind the Homestead; the day the mail plane crashed on the mountain (and how by the time a search party reached the wreck the motor had already been carted away); how Sam Snead got held back in the 6th grade because he slugged the principal, Mr. Cummins, when he tried to paddle him.

No matter what we did, it was far more than simply a kid's adventure dream come true, it was an information and experience feast.

My father was Gene's boss at the family business, the Lock Joint Pipe Company. Very recently, when I was pushing Gene for insights about my family, he somewhat reluctantly told me about his first meeting with Dad after the war. It didn't go well. Father was apparently pretty imperious, and Gene let him know in no uncertain terms he wouldn't be treated like a servant. Father got huffy, stood up, and acted as if he might throw a punch.

Gene told him he'd just come back from two years in the jungle running around with a sixty pound mortar on his back, and if Father pushed him, he'd "take him apart like a Mickey Mouse watch." Father backed down. He always told me he had the utmost respect for Gene, and Gene always said Father was among his best and most loyal friends. I think I understand the dynamics a little better now.

Gene's first job was in Wisconsin setting up a plant to make large-diameter concrete pipe. His yard foreman was having trouble getting the workers in line, so he asked the main office in New Jersey to send someone who could crack some heads. A few days later Frank Williams showed up, and immediately took charge of the situation. Soon absenteeism was down, productivity was up, and the plant was running smoothly.

Gene told Frank how pleased he was with his work, and jokingly asked if he had any brothers who might want to work for Lock Joint. Frank said he had a bunch of brothers, but with a few exceptions they were all back home, farming.

"Where's home?" Gene asked.

"In Virginia. Little place in the mountains you never heard of."

"I'm from Virginia. Maybe I know it."

"Town's called Millboro Springs. Now, I *know* you never heard of that."

"I not only know it, I grew up ten miles away from it! You wouldn't be C. J. Williams' son, would you?"

He was. And just to deepen the coincidence a bit, they were also fourth cousins.

Chapter VII

Hold The Wheel, Boy

Frank's family settled in Bath in the mid-1770's. His paternal great-grandfather fought in the Revolutionary War, and his grandfather was a physician who was killed in the Civil War. Frank was born in 1910, the fourteenth of seventeen children. The 20th century was slow to arrive in Bath, and Frank's life on the family farm was frontier-like. Everyone had a job, even the toddlers had their chores. They raised horses, cattle, sheep and poultry, and grew or hunted what they needed for food. Twice a year they loaded wagons with grain, and along with some livestock, the entire family rode fifty miles to Staunton. There they had their grain milled, and traded or sold some along with their livestock in exchange for basics like shoes, fabric, salt, sugar, coffee and tools they couldn't forge at home.

They were a self-sufficient family with a reputation for hard work and honesty. The older children were schooled at home, but the younger ones went to a one-room school through the eighth grade. On Saturday night neighbors got together to socialize, square dance and share a community supper. On Sunday they attended the nearby Windy Cove Presbyterian Church (founded in 1749), but socializing after services was limited, and did not usually include a meal. That was seen as a "picnic," an unchristian frivolity not allowed on a Sunday. Even when I was a kid in the mid-1940's, there was still a feeling among many in the community that picnics were fine on Saturday, but Sunday was for church and rest only.

Ironically, at the same time, Bath was one of only two counties where one could buy beer on Sundays. That was because Bath is on the border with West Virginia where Sunday sales were absolutely forbidden, and even when you could buy beer, it was "near beer," 3.2% watered-down stuff. Sunday sales were brisk near the state line.

Frank was eighteen when his father died. Because the farm was split up among the older boys, Frank decided to leave the county. An older brother had already established himself in the New York area, so Frank moved in with him and got a job at a local stable.

He had grown up riding, handling and caring for farm horses. Stubborn, ornery or unbroken, it didn't make a bit of difference to Frank, he could ride any of them.

Because of his skill with rough horses, Frank started riding in rodeos. He did well, earned a little money, and by the mid-1930's worked his way up to the rodeo in Madison Square Garden. He won the bronco-busting event, and walked off with a considerable cash prize. Because of his reputation as a tough cowboy on the rodeo circuit, the popular (and still published) *Wild West* magazine featured Frank on several of its covers, and he became the face of the fictional character, Tommy Rockford.

Using his prize money and proceeds from *Wild West*, he teamed up with a French Canadian friend and they opened a stable, the Rocky Hill Riding Club, in New Rochelle, New York.

Arthur Murray was a pupil; "I taught that bald-headed fart how to ride," Frank once joked. Another student was Mickey Miles, the daughter of a well-to-do and socially proper family. Her father was a widower, totally dedicated to the protection and correct

Rodeo champion Frank Williams rides a sawhorse posing as
Wild West Weekly hero, Tommy Rockford, in 1933.
(Photograph courtesy of Mrs. G. C. Williams).

upbringing of his only daughter and her two brothers. It didn't take long for a romance to develop between Mickey and Frank, and word quickly reached Mr. Miles that his darling daughter was dating a cowboy. He tried forbidding it, sent Mickey on long vacations, and threatened her—all to no avail.

Seeing that wasn't working, he hit on the genius notion of a reverse strategy: he invited Frank to a dinner dance at his country club reasoning the country rube would embarrass Mickey right out of the relationship. Frank borrowed a suit and did his best to be polite. He made it through dinner, but not knowing how to "slow dance," he had to endure a parade of young men who approached Mickey, bowed politely, and asked her to dance.

"May I have the pleasure of this dance?"

"I guess so," she said. "Is it all right, Frank?"

It was all right until the fifth or sixth time.

"May I have the pleasure of this dance?"

Frank broke. "No, you can't," he said standing up. He grabbed the startled suitor by the scruff of the neck, lifted him off the ground, and marched him across the dance floor toward the front door. Another young man tried to intervene, but Frank grabbed him with his other hand, and threw them both down the front steps. The police came, there was a terrific struggle, and Frank ended up in jail.

Mr. Miles was overjoyed, but his celebration didn't last long. Mickey bailed Frank out of jail, they paid his fine, and eloped that night.

That was the start of a loving, fifty-three-year marriage.

Frank sold his part of the stable to his partner, and took his bride home to Bath. Mickey received a message from her father threatening to cut her off completely because she married a man who, in his view, "never would amount to anything."

*Mickey Miles at Frank Williams' Rocky Hill Riding Club in
New Rochelle, New York, just before their elopement.
(Photograph courtesy of Mrs. G.C. Williams).*

In return, Frank and Mickey sent back a photograph taken up Pig Run Hollow with a group of back-woods folks, some literally wearing feed sacks, and all looking like the product of excessive closeness among siblings.

Mickey labeled the picture "My New Family," and sent it to New Rochelle. Her father immediately disinherited her. Ironically, many years later, one of Mickey's brothers finished a highly successful engineering career and retired to Bath to live near the Williams family.

The Pig Run Hollow story has a P.S. Bath County was (and still is, to some extent) isolated. The railroad only touched a tiny piece of it, and there are no major roads in and out. Pig Run is one of the most secluded parts of the county, and until recently its only road was dirt. In the 1920's (so the story goes) three large

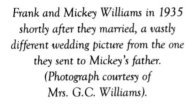

*Frank and Mickey Williams in 1935
shortly after they married, a vastly
different wedding picture from the one
they sent to Mickey's father.
(Photograph courtesy of
Mrs. G.C. Williams).*

families living up the hollow had become so inbred that the State of Virginia decided to intervene. According to Frank, Virginia Militia soldiers raided the hollow, and after a considerable fight, rounded up the worst cases, and sent them to Western State Hospital in Staunton where Dr. Joseph DeJarnette was in charge of a large eugenics program.

I recently found one descendent who lost two relatives in the raid. Though the memory is dim, he recalls them being taken and sent off to a hospital where they remained for many years.

DeJarnette graduated from the Medical College of Virginia in 1888, and immediately took the job of Third Assistant Superintendent at one of the state's large mental hospitals, Western State Hospital. By 1906 he had become Superintendent, a job in which he persisted for over fifty years. *Who's Who in America* described him as "Democrat, Presbyterian. Sponsor of sterilization law of Va., also for state care of idiots."

127

In 1869, Francis Galton published his opus, *Hereditary Genius*, in which he 'proved' the corrosive effect of bad breeding on the health of society. He envisioned a system of selective breeding and arranged marriage that would eventually produce a super race. He coined the word "eugenics" for his theory in 1883.

Eugenic theory held that propagation among the unfit produces defective, immoral, antisocial weaklings. An easy way to get started was to restrict "inferior stock" from coming into the USA. In 1926 the American Eugenics Society was founded based in large measure on the idea that the upper crust did better because of superior breeding. They argued that immigration of "inferior stock" (meaning most East Europeans, Greeks and Italians) should be shut down completely.

It doesn't take much of a leap to get to the next idea: neutralize genetically undesirable citizens by involuntary sterilization or (for the worst cases) permanent incarceration in mental hospitals. The three targeted groups were epileptics, the insane, and retarded persons. While eugenics was strongly opposed by a host of medical, religious, and some political figures, over half of the states had eugenics laws. The last survived into the 1970's.

Nowhere was it more vigorously pursued than at Western State Hospital under the firm hand of Dr. Joseph Spencer DeJarnette (supported by his wife, Chertsey, also a physician). By the time of Dr. DeJarnette's death, over 6,000 unfortunate citizens were forcibly sterilized, a shameful blot on the state's history.

Dr. DeJarnette is buried in the Warm Springs cemetery about two hundred feet from my grandparent's grave.

When my grandfather became ill in 1951, his horse-breeding operation was ended, and his sons decided to convert the farm to a cattle and sheep business. Uncle Jack had worked for the Lock Joint Pipe Company in the late 1940's. Even though he was stationed in the far-away Dominican Republic, he still felt the oppressive management hand of his two older brothers, especially when illness sidelined their father. He quit the company, moved to Bath County, and tried to run the new livestock business. Again, the brothers made life miserable for him so he (again) quit, bought a farm on the far side of the mountain, and started raising purebred Hereford cattle.

Sadly, only a few years later he was killed on Warm Springs Mountain by a run-away carnival truck carrying an enormous machine called the Rocket Ride.

Even in death Jack couldn't get away from ridicule. Being killed by a lowly carnival truck added humiliation to tragedy. It's as if Jack chose to go to heaven in a ten-cent ride.

When Jack left the farm, Gene suggested Frank Williams might be willing to take the job. Frank was well known and respected in the company, and Gene felt he had the starch to deal with the family. Frank already had some land and a house in Pig Run where he planned to retire some day.

He took the job. But he was savvy about the hazards of working for the Madam and her two older sons, so he accepted under one condition: he was the boss on the farm, wouldn't run errands, and would leave if the family tried to micro-manage him. They agreed.

Within twenty-four hours of his arrival the deal nearly fell apart.

Frank, his wife and three sons, moved into the manager's house, then paid a courtesy visit on the Madam. She was pleasant and welcoming, but as they were leaving she asked if they were registered to vote. Yes, they were.

"Good," she said. "You see, we're Republicans, and we expect our employees to vote as we do."

"Well, we're Democrats," Frank shot back, "And we expect to vote that way. I can get our things back on the truck, and we can be out of here by tomorrow morning."

The Madam immediately backed down, saying she didn't realize how strongly he felt about it, but she didn't apologize. Father and Allan begged him to stay, promising such a thing would never happen again. Frank did stay, though he and the Madam had little to say to each other after that. In fact, I can't recall Frank ever saying anything about her. She, on the other hand, often made snippy remarks about him.

The Williams family immediately became a force in my life. Their oldest son, Glenn, became—and remains—one of my closest friends. From the start, I spent as much time as I could with them. I used any excuse I could think of to get out of the main house and over to the Williams'. There was always a place for me at their table, and when I was with Frank and the boys on the farm, he inevitably had a job for me. It could be no more than holding a rope or fetching a tool, but soon became driving a tractor and stacking hay bales.

One of my favorite little moments, one that was repeated over and over, was the excitement of sitting next to Frank in a vehicle—any vehicle. A truck, a car, it didn't matter. When Frank decided it was time to roll a cigarette he'd say to whoever was sitting next to him: "Hold the wheel, boy."

Then he'd instantly let go of the wheel, reach into his pocket for rolling paper and tobacco, and roll a cigarette. He didn't slow down, and no force on earth would make him take the wheel before the cigarette was in his mouth and lit. It wasn't too scary on a dirt road on the farm, but it was a heart-stopper on the highway. Still, we never had an accident, and I'd like to think it might have made me a better driver.

Frank's wife, Mickey, was an extraordinary cook, and the house was always filled with the smell of freshly baked bread, rolls and pies. Even Father liked to sneak over for the occasional meal. During lambing and calving time in the early spring there were usually a number of orphaned or rejected lambs on the back porch and in the kitchen. There was no such thing as a specific time to start or end work, especially when there was hay to bale. And it never seemed to matter to Mickey when everyone came in from work—dinner was always ready.

Frank had a lot of kin in the area, and when the Sunday picnic taboo started to fade, we often went to one of the relative's farms for an outing after church. I especially loved Uncle Bob's place. He had a big swimming pond with a long diving board, and a place in the river where the rapids had worn the rock as smooth as glass. We climbed the hill and rode the river down to the bottom over and over until we were exhausted.

Back at Meadow Lane, Sunday usually meant a coat and tie dinner at three in the afternoon. More jellied soup. Elbows off the table, young man, this isn't some farmer's house.

Glenn and I became instant buddies. With our .22's and fishing rods, we were always on the river or up in the woods. We liked to camp out, but at first we lacked both the skills and equipment to do it comfortably. No one in my family would consider such a thing. Camping was something they were forced to do as kids at summer camp, hated it, and swore they would never again leave the comfort of their bedrooms. So for us camping was strictly learn-as-you-go, and what little equipment we had was scavenged from the barns.

Initially, our "tent" was a tarp lean-to, the top tied to a fence, the bottom anchored with rocks. We slept on the ground, two discarded horse blankets for bedding, folded jackets for pillows. Somehow, taking food with us seemed like cheating, so we relied on catching a fish. We cooked it by first wrapping the cleaned fish in several layers of wet Sycamore leaves, then pushed the wet wad into the coals of the camp fire. It was actually quite good, but we quickly found out it worked best with smaller fish. The big ones took too long to cook through, and the leaves burned up leaving chunks of partially cooked flesh clinging to hot coals.

About the third or fourth time out we had a night so thoroughly miserable we made up our minds to build a permanent camp, and equip it with the rudiments needed for at least modest comfort. It was hard for Glenn to get permission from his father to go camping. When he did, it was strictly understood he couldn't leave until his chores were done and would be back in time for morning chores. Having a permanent camp would give us more time to fish and hunt, and no time wasted in the morning packing up our stuff.

One night, before we had our permanent camp, we both remember as the worst—but in some ways the funniest—night of camping either of us has ever known. We still laugh about it. We had permission to camp out on a Saturday night. The weather was ominous. The wind was building from the southwest, always the direction for the worst storms. But the chance to go camping didn't come often so we ignored the weather.

I helped Glenn with his chores so we could get going early, set up our tarp, and have time to catch a fish. Because we knew it was going to rain, we decided to camp in the woods under a big pine, not out in an open field. We quickly put up the tarp and headed for the river to catch dinner.

Then it started to rain, and the temperature fell dramatically. There was no possible way to catch a fish in that downpour, so we trudged back toward camp, soaking wet, cold, and fishless. When we got back, our fire pit was full of water, our wood was saturated, and we couldn't find any dry wood for even a tiny fire under the tarp. Wrapped in horse blankets, we sat shivering, considering our options. Going home was tempting, but seemed to us to be admitting defeat, and we vowed to somehow make it through the night.

Then we heard the sound of food. Quack, quack, quack. Our camp was just above a wide slough, and it was full of ducks. We took a .22 and sneaked down the hill ever so carefully. After all, we were going to get just one shot, miss it and starve. Of course, we hadn't considered just how we would cook it. But that could wait. The other, more immediate, problem was how to get the duck out of the slough if we did kill it. The answer: wait until one got close enough to shore to reach it with a stick.

We waited. And waited. It was almost dark before a mallard finally drifted into range. One shot later, he was ours.

Back under the tarp we plucked it. If you've ever plucked a duck you know that even under the best of circumstances it's a messy job. The big feathers hang on tightly and the little ones are slippery. When they do come out, they stick to your fingers. But we didn't care, and with numb digits we got most of the feathers off. Then we had to face the question of how to cook it without a fire.

We had a box of kitchen matches, so we wove a miniature grill out of wet branches, cut the meat into thin strips, and held match after match under the frame until we ran out of matches. Then we ate. Every scrap. Was it good? I'd be lying if I said it was, but to us it seemed a triumph. We had beaten the rain, and had our dinner.

Next, we had to get through the night. We wrapped up as tightly as we could and tried to sleep. But we were camped on a slight incline, and the rainwater started to run through our shelter in little rivulets. We built a berm to keep the water out, but by then there was no dry ground left, the dike quickly saturated and started to leak. Our horse blankets sucked up the icy ground water like enormous lantern wicks. Even time was too cold to move at its regular pace. Seconds became minutes, minutes became hours. And the rain continued to pound the tarp just inches over our heads.

Sleep was absolutely out of the question, so to take our minds off the soggy cold we talked about how we would never, *ever*, again allow ourselves to get caught so foolishly unprepared. During the night we planned a permanent camp, one with real roof, something soft to sleep on, and room to sit up, eat and relax in the worst storm imaginable.

We showed up for chores in the morning proud we hadn't given in to the elements, and cheered by the plans for our new camp.

Soon after, we started work on what we grandly called The Williams and Hirsh Hunt Club. We scavenged some discarded boards, and with a bucket of rusty nails we went to the most remote part of the farm to build a ten-foot long box set on two large parallel downed tree trunks. We put a door on one side of the front, and some shelves inside on the other end to store our battered pot, an old frying pan, a couple of forks, and a jar of matches. The door was hinged at the top, so when it was propped open, it was like a porch roof. The support logs held the front up off the ground enough so we could sit comfortably in the wide doorway, our feet barely touching the ground. Tarpaper on the sloped roof kept it from leaking, and a couple of bales of straw under our horse blankets gave us a soft place to sleep. We had light from an old kerosene lantern hung under the open door (we had a rule: no fire inside). We fashioned a permanent stone fireplace with a metal grate for cooking, and a flue to direct the smoke away from the door. Not bad for a couple of kids.

We used the "hunt club" for years, and I credit it with doing away with any fear of the night. Shortly after we finished it we were going to use it one night, but suddenly Glenn couldn't go, and I wouldn't be able to leave until after dark. "Why don't you go alone?" asked Glenn. Why waste an opportunity for a night in the woods? "Sure, I'll go," I said bravely.

My only other solo-in-the-night experience had been several years earlier. I can't recall exactly how old I was, but I was probably six or seven. I had received a tongue lashing from Father for something, I have no idea what at this point, and I had gone to bed furious and frustrated. When he was angry there was simply no way to rebut, deflect or interrupt him. And revenge was out of the question unless it was done either surreptitiously or in a totally disguised way.

I do remember lying in the bed thinking about running away. Of course, that was totally out of the question, but how about an over-night furlough? Leave for the night, but be back before anyone missed me? Yeah, that'll work.

When the house fell silent I made my move. There was a small door in the back of my closet opening into a thirty-foot tunnel that ran across the top of the kitchen to another closet in an empty servant's suite, and an outside stair from there to the back of the house. Wearing pajamas, a robe and my sneakers, I crept out of the house and walked down the lane toward the river. It was pretty dark that night, but there was enough moonlight to see my way along without a flashlight.

It was a frightening walk, but I was more angry than scared, and totally fixed on my mission. I walked about a mile to a hay barn next to the river. Then the really scary part: going in this ancient barn, literally feeling my way along to find a sleeping place high up in the loft. But once I settled into my nest, a feeling of calm and control came over me. I slept well.

At first light I made my way back undiscovered and triumphant.

But a solo trip to the hunt club at night was different. Even though I was older and the place was quite familiar, it involved a long walk through the woods on an ill-defined trail, not a simple jaunt down an open dirt road.

I had a serious talk with myself about the irrationality of fearing the woods, dismissing the idea that the escaped madman with a hook for a hand was going to be out there waiting for me behind a tree. There were rattlesnakes up there, too, so I had to remind myself they are generally inactive at night. You can usually smell a skunk way before you stumble over him, and the black bears we had seen always ran away.

Armed with a flashlight and my .22, I walked into the woods to the camp. Honestly, I was scared witless, but I got there without being ambushed, sprayed, bitten or mauled, and calmed down when I got the fire going. By the time I was ready for sleep I was almost calm. I woke up completely relaxed, almost giddy with the feeling of triumph over what had been a major anxiety only a few hours before. I ate a bacon sandwich, closed up the camp, and walked home a new man.

When I was 14 I asked my parents if they would let me spend the summer on the farm working for Frank. To my surprise they said yes—provided the Williams would have me. With my heart in my throat I asked them, and to my amazement they said yes.

But there were conditions. First, the wages were three dollars a day. Second, I had to live with the Williams, and that meant no contact with my parents or any trips to the main house. No dinners or socializing with the family, no vacation with them, no time off or anything beyond the occasional phone call, or a chat if we ran into each at the barn or along the road. If I got sick or needed to go to the doctor for stitches, the Williams would take care of it.

"If you work for me, you're a Williams." Frank's rules: simple and unambiguous.

I jumped at it, and as soon as school was out, I moved in. Glenn, his brother, Dennis, and I lived in a one-room cabin—once a chauffeur's "house"—next to the manager's house. Three beds, three bureaus, a bathroom with a sink, toilet and a coffin-like tin shower. One bare bulb hung from the ceiling, and the front porch had two old rickety chairs facing the barn. It was heaven.

The day started at 6:00AM. After breakfast we milked the cows, then piled into Frank's pick-up, and joined the other farm hands to get our orders. By lunch we were so tired we mindlessly wolfed something down then fell asleep on the couch or the floor until Frank yelled it was time to go. At the end of the day, we milked the cows again, then went back to the Williams' house, hungry and exhausted. There was no TV, and even if there had been, no one would have watched it. We were asleep a half an hour after evening chores and dinner were out of the way.

A day with Frank was a lot more than muscle and endurance building. He wouldn't have acknowledged it, but Frank was a perpetual teacher. He talked about what he was doing when he tore down an engine, welded a broken part or primed a trash pump. And after he explained it once he expected us to do it from then on. There was a certain way to stack hay bales on a wagon so they wouldn't fall off going up a steep hill. There was a particular knot to use on a horse's lead, a certain way to cut the end of a dynamite fuse so it would light instantly, and a way to bend a fist full of downed hay to tell if it was dry enough to bale.

Being with Frank was learning big lessons from little details, and finding out you could always push yourself a little more, a little harder, a little further than you thought you could. It was about a new definition of pain, and what constituted an injury. When I scraped all the skin off my knuckles using a pinch bar too close to a fence, Frank said to let it bleed, that way it would clean itself and I could keep on working. "Keep it clean, keep it out of your mouth, and it'll heal up just fine." And it did.

When Dennis sliced his leg open with a chain saw, Frank's comment was something about seeing all that "fat meat." Glenn remembers his father saying "We'll see about that at lunch." Either way, there was no hysteria, no sense of panic. It was simply another problem to be solved. The wound was worth a good twenty stitches, but Frank simply washed it out, pulled the edges together with tape, bound it up tightly, and sent Dennis back to work. It healed perfectly well.

We rarely wore gloves and blisters were common. Once, when we were pounding stakes with a sledgehammer, I got five or six fat blisters. At lunch Frank poked a hole in each with his penknife, then rubbed salt in my palm. It hurt like hell for a few minutes, but sure enough, they dried out, and I kept on pounding. Not only did the hand heal quickly, but the dried blisters thickened into durable calluses, like having on permanent gloves. No more blisters.

During that summer we put up 22,000 bales of hay; built an enormous fish pond with a large clay and rock dam; took apart and reassembled the rear end of a giant D-9 Caterpillar bulldozer; harvested 400 acres of corn, oats and barley; de-horned close to one hundred steers; and took 200 or so lambs and calves to market.

When I think back to my early summers, that one stands out as the most remarkable of them all. I have no way to measure the carpentry, machine, animal, and mechanical skills I learned from Frank, and I still use them all. But far more important than knowing how to use dynamite or drive a ten-penny nail through an oak board, the experience changed my way of thinking.

Because of the no-contact-with-parents rule, I was quite invisible to the family that summer. Yet I was among them all the time watching, but not interacting beyond a casual wave or quick hello. To me, they all seemed trapped in their routine. While they lived on the farm, their focus was on golf and tennis at the Homestead, cocktails at the so-in-so's, or perhaps an elaborate picnic at the river.

We never saw them in the hay field, at the barns, or at the swimming hole. While I was having the time of my life in sweaty blue jeans, soaking up new experiences, hearing music and meeting the people who lived around us, my parents remained stuck in their gabardine tar baby. They could have and do anything they wanted, yet what they chose—and demanded their intimates choose along with them—seemed to limit their options, especially when it came to exploring the natural richness surrounding them.

Invisible as I was to the family, I was equally so in the community. I had temporarily lost my identity as a Hirsh and had become a Williams. Every day I was in the feed store, the mill, at Webb's or the livestock market. I went to the local church, was part of every Williams family gathering, picnic or square dance. People didn't notice me, much less hold back or censor any of their thoughts.

And what did I hear about "us?" Nothing. Zero. We weren't disliked, ridiculed or criticized, and we certainly weren't envied or admired. None of the above. The Hirshs had chosen not to be part of the community, and the community didn't care one way or the other. It shrugged its shoulders and went on working.

To hear my parents on the subject was to think everyone around was drooling to be like us, own a duck press, a split bamboo fly rod, and a set of Harrod's croquet mallets. T'wern't so. What an eye opener!

Before that summer in the Williams' home, to the extent I thought about my future at all, it seemed to be already mapped out by the family. There was a plan, I would follow it, and as long as I more-or-less got through my education I would end up an engineer at Lock Joint, play a lot of golf and probably own a horse or two— even if I didn't like to ride.

But the message from Frank, echoing what Gene had been saying for years, was just the opposite: if you stick to blind dependence on family-generated assumptions—no matter how comfortable they make you—and allow prejudice to shape relationships, you will pay a hefty price. Neither man was consciously trying to say anything. It was simply who they were and what they did. The example of their own relationships spoke with total clarity. Their lives were visceral, tactile, full of humor and open to new ideas. Their marriages worked, their relationships with their children, family and friends were real and functional.

Both of my heroes were tough as nails, at times stern and demanding, and neither tolerated excuses, whining or any hint of dishonesty. Both could be scary, especially if you stepped over some forbidden boundary. While Father's brand of 'scary' made me fearful and angry, Frank's and Gene's generated respect and a wish to do better. The difference was obvious, even to an adolescent kid.

My parents deserve a lot of credit for giving me time with both families, and not interfering even slightly with my summer with the Williams. It was easily one of the greatest gifts they ever gave me, even though they had no idea what a profound and lasting effect it would have on me.

The Williams worked on Meadow Lane Farm for twenty-five years. They retired to their place in Pig Run, and raised cattle until Frank was too old and ill to handle it any longer. In 1985 Frank and Mickey celebrated their fiftieth anniversary. About two hundred friends came from around the country to help celebrate. There was an endless supply of food, kids running all over the place, and people who hadn't seen each other in a long time hugged and laughed.

At one point Frank was sitting on a picnic table off to one side of the gathering. He rolled a cigarette, took a long tug, and chuckled.

"What's so funny, Frank?" someone asked.

"Oh, I was just thinkin'," Frank said nodding toward the crowd. "It's not bad for someone who wasn't supposed to amount to anything."

About ten years later Frank developed cancer. Before long it spread, eventually reaching his brain. He became weaker, and increasingly limited in what he could do. He spent his days in a recliner in the living room, unable to move back and forth to the bedroom. The last time I saw him, it took him a while to recognize me.

"What are you doing here, boy?"

"I came to see you."

"Ain't much to see," he said with a weak smile. Then he closed his eyes.

Mickey was not well herself. She had suffered severe asthma attacks all her life. As she grew older the attacks became more debilitating and harder to get through. I always remember a giant green oxygen tank in her room, and the scary sound she made when she had an episode. They often struck at night, but Frank was always there to get her medicine, hook her up to the oxygen system, and see her through the attack.

Shortly after my last visit, Frank's condition worsened, and he fell into a coma. During the night, Mickey had an asthma attack. Frank roused from his coma, went into the bedroom, got her medicine, started the oxygen, and sat with her until she fell asleep.

In the morning Frank was back in his chair in the living room. He had passed away in the night.

I didn't learn of his death until just after his funeral. Ironically, I was driving to the farm from Baltimore, and as we passed the Windy Cove Church we saw a huge number of cars—far more than one would see even on Easter Sunday—and a hearse.

"Must be the funeral of somebody awfully important," my wife said.

A few hours later we found out she was right. My parents knew of Frank's death right after it happened, but didn't bother to let me know. I was livid, and confronted Father about it. His response was a shrug.

"I can't be responsible for letting you know every little thing that goes on around here."

Uncle Gene is now in his eighties, has a couple of metal knees, and takes something "damned expensive" to control his leukemia.

Aunt Mary Jean, his wife of over fifty years, died recently. She had Alzheimer's Disease for a number of years and over time had become mute. Gene refused to consider placing her in a nursing home despite the enormous demands of her care. Toward the end he had some help from visiting nurses, but he continued to insist she be cared for at home.

In spite of the devastation caused by her dementia, her death was a surprise. Gene is glad she was able to stay at home, and never seemed the least resentful of the weight of her illness. He was particularly gratified to be able to protect her dignity, and see to it that her hygiene and dress were always as she would have wanted it.

"She always looked so pretty," he said. "Right up to the day she died."

Gene has sold his house in Florida and moved back to Bath, "Coming home," he calls it. Sometimes we get to go fishing. The last time we went, we stood in the riffles of the Jackson River "drowning worms," as he likes to say, doing more talking than fishing. The breeze was stirring the late-afternoon fragrance of the meadow and river, and around us, the birds, bugs and frogs all seemed to have something to say.

"Think about it," Gene said, "Sixty years later, and we're still in the river. Either we're the worst damn fishermen in the world or there's something magic about this place."

Magic, indeed. I ask myself: how can one person be this lucky? Pure dumb luck again.

Chapter VIII

Paradise Temporarily Lost

On May 7, 1945, the family huddled around a Hallicrafters short wave radio in the music room in my grandparent's house at Meadow Lane Farm. Through the crackle and static we heard the news: Germany had surrendered! Like millions of families around the country we cried, hugged, and celebrated wildly. If they didn't send him to the Pacific, Uncle Allan would soon be home!

Japan would surely follow, the war would be over for everyone, and life would return to normal. I expected a summer with Miss Hite, Jim Sally and Dasher. Perfect!

Well, not so perfect. Miss Hite was really Mrs. Hite, and the railroad had transferred her husband out of the area. Then, back in Montclair, a man named Doc Ellsworth paid us a visit. He brought a 16mm film projector and showed us the glories of Camp Calumet in Ossipee, New Hampshire, where—lucky me—I would spend the first two months of the summer. The fact I didn't want to go had nothing to do with it. When I asked my mother years later why she had shipped me off at the tender age of seven, she said it was because I had "too much ego," and camp would be good for me, a character-building experience. Make new friends. Learn to swim.

I already had friends and I could swim perfectly well. Besides, who will ride Jim Sally while I'm away?

"The grooms will. And when you get home from camp, you can ride to your heart's content."

I was doomed.

A DC-3 filled with campers left Newark Airport in early June. We landed in Boston, transferred to yellow school buses, and after three nauseating hours, arrived at Lake Ossipee and Camp Calumet. Along the way, counselors stood swaying in the aisles teaching us the camp song (tune stolen from Cornell's college song), the camp cheer (Boom-Chigga-Boom, Boom-Chigga-Boom...), and the Rules.

And there were plenty of Rules. First off, we must never, ever cross the camp boundaries. Second, no bad language, and we're not talking the S or the F words here. Bad language included "damn," "piss" and "crap." Third, a counselor's word is law. You will obey.

Then there was the visitation rule. That one was quite simple: if you were there for only one month, no visitors. If you were a lifer like me, condemned to two months, one two-hour visit was allowed during shift change at the end of one month. You can receive mail, but no candy or money allowed. On Sunday, after dinner, every camper was allowed a candy bar from the "store" in the dining hall. Some store, it was open for ten minutes a week.

Dress was simple: shorts, tank top, sneakers and socks. Maybe underwear took too much rationed soap, I don't know, but underwear was not allowed.

And then there were the counselors, most just back from fighting the war in Europe. They were hard as nails, loud, and some were downright sadistic. I suppose it's asking a lot to go from a foxhole to summer camp in a matter of weeks, but some of them should have made an intermediate stop in a psychiatric facility before taking on 200 kids.

As the busses rumbled across the little bridge into camp, the order went out for the camp cheer. Boom Chigga Boom, we're finally here. We were marched straight-away to the dining hall to write a post card home telling our parents how much fun we had on the trip up. If anyone was stuck, counselors had a supply of easy sentences already prepared.

After the cards were collected, we went to our assigned cabins. Camp was divided into three sections. Lower Camp (cabins 1-6), Middle Camp (cabins 7-12), and Upper Camp (all tents, for seniors.) I don't remember, but I'll bet seniors were allowed underwear. Along with eight other seven-year-olds, I was in Cabin One, absolutely the lowest and most remote of all cabins. It was literally on the bank of a swamp, thought (wrongly, as it turned out) to be the only boundary line no camper would ever try to cross.

Cabin One at Camp Calumet, 1945.
Author at age 7; back row, left, ready to become a resistance fighter.

Each cabin was a one-room box. The two counselors, mindful of every move we made, slept by the door. Because we were so far from the lower camp latrine, there was fear we would—out of laziness—urinate in the swamp. That and a whole bunch of other offenses would earn punishment ranging from detention all the way up to a trip to Doc Ellsworth's office and (shudder) possible expulsion.

Every day began with a trip to a large assignment board on the end of the all-purpose building, a cavernous place for rainy-day activities, grudge-generated boxing matches, and sometimes a movie. One moved about from Leather Shop, to Wood Shop, to Metal Shop, or to Swim, Sailing, or Canoe Class. Each was highly structured, and designed to give you a skill or product to take home. No bird houses in Wood Shop: won't fit in your trunk. You will make a ship silhouette. I expected to be making license plates in Metal Shop, but instead we ground out metal ashtrays. Everyone in the lower camp made a belt of interlocking leather loops, and a lanyard to hold a key none of us had.

Don't be fooled by the sailing and canoeing thing, either. For the lowlifes, sailing meant cramming a half dozen kids into a Lightening to drift aimlessly in front of the camp taking turns holding the limp jib sheet. And don't call it a rope or a line. That'll cost you.

The canoes were only for upper campers. Same for the row boats. Just wait until you're a Middle! You can take a canoe out by yourself! Wow. I can't wait.

We ate by cabin group, a counselor at either end of the table watching our manners. In the middle of the table, a little green slotted block of wood held a card listing our names. If one spoke out of turn, rested an elbow on the table, or used a utensil improperly, one of the counselors penciled a strike next to your name. At the conclusion of the Sunday mid-day meal, the strikes were tallied, and the kid with the fewest marks was given a reward: an extra bowl of ice cream.

It was obvious none of these guys had ever had dinner with the Madam, because at the end of the first week I had no strikes at all. Congratulations! A landslide winner! The rest of the kids fled leaving one lone child at each table to savor his prize. We ate in silence, watched by a counselor. I was given ice cream with nuts in it. I hate ice cream with nuts. And I had to eat it all; the starving children thing was fresh and real in 1945. No one left a scrap of anything.

When I finished my ice cream and went out for Free Time, the teams were already made up and playing, every horseshoe pit was taken, and there were no seniors left to let you ride in the bottom of a canoe. The meal winners sat around and watched the others play.

That was the last time I let myself be hoodwinked by the manners scam. From then on I watched the card ever so carefully, and if it looked like I might be getting the lead, I put both elbows on the table and burped.

I quickly found out there were other cons, too. And, yes, one was the proverbial Snipe Hunt.

Everyone jokes about the snipe hunt, it's imbedded in our lexicon. It means any outrageous con or trick perpetrated on a young and hopelessly naïve subject; for example, a 1945 city kid who had never spent any time on a farm.

It started one evening right after dinner before the first horseshoe was thrown. There was no warning; suddenly, the counselors were racing around the lower camp telling everyone we were going to have a snipe hunt for all the new campers. Bring your flashlight and gather at the baseball field, snipe have been spotted in the woods!

When we got to the field we were divided into teams of three. One kid was the light man, one was the "caller," and one was the bag man. They put us just inside the woods in a long line perhaps five yards apart facing into the forest. The bagman held the sack open, the light man shone his light in the bag, and the caller clicked two rocks together: click-click-clickclickclick. The synchronous snipe-calling Morse code droned on for what seemed like forever.

Our team wasn't fooled by any of this, but the counselors rushed up and down the line encouraging everyone to stay on his toes. These New Hampshire snipe are really fast. Then suddenly there was a great commotion in the woods in front of us. Counselors were on a "drive" to chase the wily birds into our traps. Then there was a blur as a counselor rushed over us, and something huge and alive was in our bag!

The whistle blew. "They got one! All in! All in!" Everyone gathered around us in a huge circle shining lights on our jumping, squawking bag. Sounds mighty much like a chicken, I thought. A counselor reached in the bag and pulled out a fat hen. He waved it briefly in the air and shoved it back in the bag.

"That's a chi…" was all I got out before the counselor had his hand over my mouth. "Don't be a wise guy," he said in my ear. Got it. A snipe. The next day, of course, the secret was out, and we were supposed to feel like fools.

It was pretty benign compared to some Calumet hazing. Another one was the Ghost of Pine Point con. That one really did scare some of the kids.

One of the few really interesting things we did was take an overnight canoe trip to Pine Point about five miles by water from the camp. There were no sleeping bags in those days, and all we had was a blanket to roll up in. That was enough to make sure no one slept a wink, but just to be sure they threw in a long and vivid campfire ghost story right before bed called (what else?) the Ghost of Pine Point. Like his cousins, Fee-Fi-Fo-Fum and Hook Man, this ghost liked to pick on children, and his specialty was half-frozen kids with no underwear.

According to the counselors they lose one or two of the smaller campers every year. We all "slept" on top of each other, no one wanting to have his feet exposed or be too near the edge of the pile. In some ways it was adaptive: at least sleeping in a wad conserved heat.

To me, Calumet was less about camping than it was adapting to adversity. Clearly, there was a gray zone between the extremes of submission and rebellion. The trick was to find that sweet spot—no easy task—to preserve your sense of personal control but avoid even the slightest visible hint of mutiny. Impulsively blowing the snipe/ chicken scam was right on the edge of too much. And stepping over the line a little further could get you in serious hot water.

And Calumet punishments were no joke, the horror of expulsion was too great to risk.

Ask my friend Andy, for example. He said the "d" word one day, and was dragged off to the counselor's shower to have his mouth washed out with soap. He didn't take it well, and before long he was declared an habitual offender and expelled. A car was brought into the camp, his trunk loaded up, and away he went. Oh, the shame of it.

I was already well schooled in the fine art of not making mistakes in my own home camp, so handling a few psychotic counselors was relatively easy. In fact, my only brush with doom was an accident entirely of some one else's manufacture. One of my fellow cabin-mates, Tony, somehow found a heavy metal rasp, and for some stupid reason hit and shattered a porcelain drinking cup on top of an outlet on the side of the infirmary. He dropped the rasp and ran just as I came around one side of the infirmary, and a counselor came around the other.

We met at the broken cup, and you can easily guess the rest. I was dragged off to Doc Ellsworth's office, pre-tried and convicted of crimes against Calumet. Ellsworth was furious, and demanded a complete confession. I protested my innocence, and he threatened to send me home. Go ahead, I don't want to be here anyway. Seeing that wasn't working, he came up with another threat: either confess now and take your punishment, or after dinner tonight I will put you over my knee, pull down your pants, and spank you in front of my office as the entire camp marches by. I held firm, but I have to tell you, I was scared he would do it.

I didn't eat that night, and when dinner was over I walked out with the others, but my knees were shaking. Ellsworth was no where in sight. That was the end of it, and all it cost was one strike on the manners card for leaving food on my plate.

The Ellsworth incident was instructive. It put me in a different place mentally. It confirmed in the most graphic way what I already knew: the place was run by lunatics, and my job was to resist without getting hurt. And if the drinking cup incident wasn't enough, the Tennis Tournament completed my conversion into a resistance fighter.

It was announced that every camper would be participating in a three-tiered tennis tournament to decide a Lower, Middle and Senior tennis champion. No exceptions. I had never played a game of tennis in my life, had not the slightest knowledge of the rules or even how to hold a racket. Too bad, I was told. *You must play.* So at the appointed hour I was given a racket and told where to stand. The kid on the other side was experienced and smacked ball after ball by me. After each point I was moved to the next position to either watch a winner go by, or take a futile stab at a return. When it was my turn to serve, the only balls I actually hit either went into the net or over the backstop.

But they wouldn't stop the massacre. Six games had to be played, and that was all there was to it. I tried my best not to cry, but when it was finally over, I took to the woods, cried, and thought about my options. I was already one of the nine youngest kids in camp. My biggest fear was that word would go out that I was also an utter incompetent, and I would be laughed at by everyone in camp.

But I hadn't broken down on the court, and in my seven-year-old naïve way I thought that perhaps when the winners were announced that night (as they were every night until the three grand winners were anointed), I would at least get recognition as a good sport.

Of course, that didn't happen. Fortunately, I wasn't ridiculed, either. No one seemed to notice. But with six weeks or so left in my summer incarceration, I somehow had to devise a way to feel back in control.

There were two currencies in the camp: comic books sent from home and candy. I had and traded as many comics as anyone, so the focus had to be on candy, and the camp maintained rigid control of that commodity. Besides, there was absolutely no money in circulation. Even if one had money, no one in camp would want it, and the nearest store—a little grocery—was a mile away. Rumor had it that some of the seniors with forbidden coin sometimes sneaked out there and weren't ratted out by the storekeeper.

So what I needed was money. The counselors had money, but no matter how desperate the situation, I would never be able to steal. That was below contempt, the act of a thug with no imagination or finesse. No, stealing was out. It had to be found some other way.

That led me to the counselor's shower. Actually, under the shower. The shower and dressing area had a slatted floor to let the water run out straight into the sand below. No pipes, no drain. If water could go through, a stray coin falling from a pocket in the dressing area could do likewise. The shower was on the edge of the camp near our cabin, its back side against the woods. By circling around through the woods I could make an invisible approach. Then I wiggled under the building into the shallow crawl space.

Bingo! By sifting the sand through my fingers I found coins. Not a fortune, mind you, but enough to buy plenty of candy.

Next step: an undetected round trip to the candy store. Fortunately, the store was located on the same side of camp as Cabin One, beyond the swamp and across a wide hay field. No road to cross until the last second.

I took my clothes off behind the cabin, put the coins in a sock, socks in my sneakers, and wrapped it all together in a tight bundle. Then, holding my clothing wad in one hand, I slipped into the swamp and half swam, half crawled through the muddy slough to the spot where the swamp met the lake, and the water was clean. It was an exposed spot, but by lying in the water I could wash off the mud without being seen from the camp. I slithered into the hay field, dressed and ran crouched over up to the road. Then I crossed the road to the back of the store. I didn't dare walk in the front door. What if there was a counselor at the counter? Happily, the store owner thought the whole thing was terribly funny, and I retraced my steps back to camp with several bars of treasure.

The trickiest part was getting the mud off at the other end. A tiny stream fed the swamp, and by crawling past the cabin I could get into clearer water, wash off the mud, dress and make it back to the cabin undetected.

I made that trip a number of times and was never caught.

I wasn't as lucky with my conversion to Catholicism. Being a do-right place meant going to church on Sunday. A nondenominational service of sorts was held in the activity building, and on the first Sunday I was there with everyone else. Well, almost everyone else. Some of the kids went off in a truck (Boom Chigga Boom), and when they came back I noticed my friend Andy had what looked like ice cream on his upper lip. Yep, sure enough, after church in town, every kid was treated to an ice cream cone.

"I'm Catholic," Andy explained. "We have to go to a real church." And afterward they got ice cream.

A minute later I was in Doc Ellsworth's office complaining I hadn't been allowed to go to church. "I didn't know you were Catholic," Ellsworth said.

The next Sunday I was in the truck with Andy. Boom Chigga Boom, and we were off to church. By doing everything Andy did, I managed not to stand out. And, yes! We got ice cream on the way back.

The scam worked for three weeks, then came the four-week change and visits. My parents arrived, but I wasn't there. Father demanded to know where I was, and when he found out, he exploded. When I got back, I was busted, and most of our two-hour visit was taken up with Father blasting me for going to the Catholic church. He didn't mind the deception—the ice cream thing made sense to him—but the idea of my being in a Catholic church sent him over the edge. So I finished the last four weeks of my sentence as a non-denominational camper. At least I had plenty of candy.

After a few days at home, I went back to the farm. But sadly, Miss Hite was gone, my parents stayed in New Jersey, and I was trapped in the house with my grandparents. The grooms rode with me, but there were no songs and little conversation. Toward the end of the summer my riding skills, rudimentary as they were, were good enough to allow me to ride alone as long as I stayed more-or-less within eyesight of the barns.

All told, it was less than a fabulous summer. Next year would be better. But in the spring, Doc Ellsworth showed up again with his movie projector, and in June—in spite of my protests—I was sent up the creek for another eight-week tour.

This time it was Cabin Three. A few of the Cabin One boys were back, and the candy scam still worked, but I only made the trip a couple of times. It was harder to get under the shower, and Cabin Three's exposed position away from the creek made it too risky. Being a little older let us swim further out in the lake, and I brought a fishing pole that summer. But it was still pretty harsh and very competitive. The older campers picked on us regularly, and by break time I was ready to go AWOL.

That year, Father came up to visit with another close family friend, "Uncle" Ermil Miller. His nickname was "Airmail Miller," because he had been a pilot in the Pacific for four years, and like Uncle Gene, had gone to work for my grandfather when he came home.

But just *how* he came home was the most remarkable part.

At the end of the war, he arrived on the west coast prepared to take a train home to the east coast. There were thousands of war planes piling up on the coast, and like many pilots, he was given one, and told to fly it to a field in Arizona where it would be

"Uncle" Ermil Miller and an SNJ like the one he flew to strafe
Camp Calumet. (Photograph of Ermil Miller courtesy of Mrs. Loretta Miller;
SNJ photograph courtesy of Mr. Michael O'Leary, Challenge Publications).

stored in the dry desert. The plane was a two-seat SNJ Navy trainer, the kind with a glass canopy that slides back to allow one pilot in front, the other in back. After dropping the plane off, Ermil was supposed to catch a bus or a train home.

Somewhere between Los Angeles and Phoenix, Ermil made a left turn and flew home in his new plane. At least that's the story I was told. No matter how he did it, Ermil had a Navy plane, and he took me on several rides. There was one outing, however, that stands out above all others, a kid's dream come true.

We were flying over Montclair, Ermil telling me over the earphones to look at this or that. "Where's your school?" he asked. When we spotted it, he said "Reach under the seat, grab the funnel." There was a funnel connected to a tube. "Want to take a leak on the school? Go ahead."

He then rolled the plane over and made a screaming pass over the school. And I let go. I'm certain not a molecule hit Brookside, but the satisfaction was enormous.

That summer, Ermil flew Father up to visit during the break. We were to have a field event that afternoon after visiting was over and the new kids had arrived. There was an enormous open field with dozens of stations through which one had to pass to get through it all. One went from the sack race to the egg-on-the-spoon race to the three-legged race, etc. The older kids resented being paired with younger kids, and delighted in squashing us in one-on-one races. I dreaded it.

I whined about it to Father and Ermil, and as they were leaving, Ermil said "You tell those kids I don't like it one bit that they pick on you. And you tell 'em I mean business: I'm going to buzz this place."

I did tell everyone I was sick and tired of being pushed around, and I had asked my uncle to strafe the place to make the point. Of course, I was laughed at. Fools, they fell right into the trap.

155

Reluctantly graduating from Jim Sally to Little Oscar.

Not long after, I heard the plane. So did everyone else, and all the games stopped as everyone looked up. Ermil flew over the field at perhaps a thousand feet, then went into a steep climb, rolled over and headed straight at us. It was right out of the Movietone newsreels we had all watched throughout the war, and everyone, including counselors, took off.

The plane screamed over the field only a few hundred feet off the deck. The noise was deafening, and the after-effect of wind literally bent the pine trees. He pulled up in another steep climb, rolled over and made a second run, this time even lower.

I stood alone in the middle of the field, waving as Ermil made a final pass, dipped his wings and flew away. I had no more difficulties in camp that year.

But back at home, it was the same as the year before: I was sent to the farm with my grandparents. Worse, Jim Sally and Dasher had been sold and the pony cart retired. Father later hung it in the stairwell of one of the houses on the farm. It's still there.

Because I was taller and could easily handle the pony, I was ready for a horse, a fourteen-hander I named Little Oscar. Now at least I was gender savvy.

On my first ride, Little Oscar ran away with me. I was terrified, but managed to hang on all the way back to the barn, including a leap over a closed gate. I have been a reluctant rider ever since.

The following spring I was 9, and damned if Ellsworth didn't show up again. This time I pitched a fit, but my parents stood firm. Ellsworth promised me a bed in Cabin Seven, the first cabin in Middle camp. OK, if I have to go, at least I won't have to be in the Lower camp.

When we arrived (Boom Chigga Boom), I was stunned to find myself in Cabin Five! Betrayed! Worse, it was not even Cabin Six. At least then, after two years of torment, I would have been in the top spot in Lower camp. Even worse, none of my old pals were back, and we had the two most sadistic counselors in camp. They ruled with an iron hand, and their punishments were draconian. Any individual infraction was punished collectively. The first time someone broke a rule, they got us up in the middle of the night, marched us to the baseball field, and flashlight in hand, made us "run the bases." I don't remember how long we did it, but it seemed like forever.

But that was nothing compared to the second punishment. Again they woke us up in the middle of the night, only this time we had to walk out into the lake in our pajamas and stand up to our necks in the cold water. By then I was a broken creature. Not one candy run that summer. Far too risky. I put in my time, and waited. Toward the end I developed a rash on my face, and when I got home I was rushed off to the doctor. Diagnosis: impetigo, a dangerous and highly contagious Strep infection associated with a lack of cleanliness.

A dirty camp! My parents, especially my mother, were livid, and it was declared then and there I would definitely *not* be sent back to Camp Calumet. If it took getting a potentially fatal disease to get away from Calumet, I was only too glad to suffer it.

Boom Chigga Boom, Ellsworth.[14]

Things were also better in Bath. That summer, we stayed in my Grandmother's house on her farm for a few weeks before camp, and for six weeks after. I was almost ten and those few weeks were not only joyous and enlightening, but introduced me to people who would stay with me a lifetime.

And one, Granny Cleek, would literally start me on a course that would lead to a career in medicine.

Chapter IX

Granny Cleek

The Madam's 1,500-acre farm was called Folly Farm, so named because she bought it impulsively, in a fit of pique generated by her anger at my grandfather. Because his business had flourished and become global, he was in the habit of making prolonged visits to his various foreign operations. In the days before WW II, that sort of travel was usually made by boat, making a "simple" trip to South America at least a month-long undertaking.

One of his favorite cities was Bogotá, Colombia. Each time he went he stayed longer and longer, well beyond the time needed to check in on company business. The Madam's suspicions grew in proportion to the length of his absence, until she finally snapped and decided she had to do something about it. So she bought her own farm and moved her horses, sheep and furniture into Folly.

When Grandfather finally came home he tried to woo her back with promises, and an enormous Colombian emerald. Not placated, she reportedly threw the emerald away. When she died, the scavenging sons searched in vain for it. Did she toss it? Or was one faster than the others? We'll never know.

They settled down into a two-house routine after that, though ninety percent of the time she stayed with Grandfather at Meadow Lane—in separate bedrooms. We moved into Folly Farm with a staff of three and I hardly saw the Madam at all that summer.

Folly Farm is at the end of a small, paved secondary road. The house is on the Jackson River, but the farm itself extends several miles up a long hollow. A twisting dirt road leads up past barns and a tenant's house, through a steep, narrow gorge, then dead-ends in a high, open plateau surrounded by mountains. About two-thirds of the way up, another tenant's house is tucked in a small opening off a steep curve. Folly Farm ends at the edge of Granny Cleek's place near the end of the twisting dirt road just past a graveyard, some abandoned sheds, and a tumbled-down schoolhouse.

The Madam employed two families at Folly: the Bryants and the Ailstocks. The Bryants, Mary, Carlos (pronounced Car-lus) and their sons Whimpy and George, lived in the first tenant's house a few hundred yards up the hollow from the main house. The Ailstocks lived on the steep curve. Mary Bryant was Granny Cleek's daughter, and worked for Grandmother in her kitchen when she was in residence at Folly. Carlos managed the farm, helped by James Ailstock and sometimes by June Cleek, Mary's brother, who lived with Granny and ran their farm at the end of the hollow. During haying season, Dizzy Dean—the cussingest man who ever walked—was also brought in to help.

Because the fields were so hilly and steep, tractor-drawn hay balers couldn't be used, so hay was put up in haystacks, and the raking and hauling of hay shocks was done by horses.

When I need to smile, I only have to think back to haying season at Folly that summer, after my final stretch at Camp Calumet. After the hay was cut, the work horses, Petunia and Begonia, pulled the hay rake around to build long "win'rows," ribbons of hay two or three feet wide and equally tall. Then men walked the rows with pitch forks building "hay shocks," miniature hay stacks about

Petunia and Begonia strut their stuff in a 1945 horse show.

five or six feet tall. When that was done, George and I climbed on Petunia and Begonia and rode bareback hauling the shocks to the stack pole, a long, tapered pole set in the ground around which the stack was built.

To haul shocks, a pole about ten feet long was attached to the traces behind the horses. It was about three inches thick where it attached to the harness, and had a rope, about as long as the pole, tied about a foot down the shaft. The pole was curved, tapered to a point, and as smooth as glass. To connect up you rode the horse as close to the shock as possible without hitting it, always in the direction of the growing stack, and stopped immediately in front of the shock. Sometimes you had to back the horse, but if you did it just right the man on the ground could grab the pole and slide it under the shock, its curve preventing it from stubbing in the ground. Then the drag rope was thrown over the shock, wrapped

Haystacks, from an old post card.

around the pole, a slipknot was tied, and the shock was hauled to the stack. Done correctly, there wasn't a bit of hay left where the shock had been, and no hay was lost dragging it to the stack.

At the stack, the builder pointed to the exact place he wanted the shock, and as you dragged it over that spot, he pulled the rope, untying the knot; the pole slipped out, and the shock was positioned in exactly the right place.

It's surprising just how much craft went into building a haystack. Each fork-full of hay was layered on so the entire stack was laced together in a tight, invisible spiral. As the stack grew, the builder switched to a long-handled, three-pronged fork, twisting the handle to slap the small, final bunches of hay together at the top. Done right, the strongest wind couldn't blow off the hay, and the stack would stand straight through the harshest winter. The weave was so tight rain couldn't penetrate to spoil the hay; instead, it ran off like an English thatch roof.

June Cleek and Carlos Bryant were our stackers. Recently, I asked June (who was 86 and still farming the Cleek place) what the secret of building a perfect stack was. "Keep your middle full, lace it tight, and don't build over twenty-five feet tall." As the stack rose the center always had to be higher and tighter than the outside. Even as hay was later gradually removed, its rain-shedding taper protected the hay all the way to the ground.

George and I spent hours and hours hauling hay shocks. When we were near the edge of a field where apple trees overhung the fence, we could sometimes snag an apple to throw at each other. No one seemed to mind as long as we kept the shocks straight and dropped them at exactly the right spot.

Petunia and Begonia were entirely placid and well trained. One hardly needed the reins, they responded instantly to voice commands. "Gee" to turn right, "Haw" for left, "Whoa" or "Back" to stop or back up, and a simple clicking sound to start. And they never shied at a sudden noise, or seemed to notice the occasional apple bouncing off their rump.

It's a little hard to put in words, but what I felt went way beyond the enormous fun of riding and hauling hay shocks. I was nine, and I think it was the first time in my life I was doing legitimate work with adults who weren't simply tolerating me, or pretending I was doing something helpful. George and I fit in with everyone else. We had our job, we were expected to do it right, and that's all there was to it. We worked the same day as everyone else, and when we sat down to eat, I was simply part of the group, one of the men. Nothing else. When there was work I could do, I got up early, and made damn sure I was where I was supposed to be right on time.

Frost comes early to Bath, sometimes at the end of August. With all the hay baled or stacked, it was time to harvest the corn and put it in the silos as silage, or, as it was known in Bath, "enslige." Most of the corn was cut off at the ground mechanically, bundled by hand, and put on wagons. Any stalks missed in the corners or on steep places were chopped using either a hand-held corn cutter similar to a short sickle with a long handle, or with a shoe cutter. The shoe cutter is a short, sharp, curved blade attached to one's boot. The stalk was dropped with a simple kick. It was a dangerous instrument, one the men used with caution. Tripping or kicking too close to someone else could be messy.

The bundled corn was taken by wagon to the silo where it was put on a short conveyor belt feeding a grinder powered by a long belt attached to a tractor. The tractor's "power take-off" powered most of the grinders, saws, and other large farm machines. The belt between the PTO and the grinder was about six inches wide, perhaps 15 feet long, and undulated up and down as it tore along at a tremendous speed. It was a very dangerous piece of equipment, especially when people ducked under it to get to the other side to avoid walking all the way around the tractor.

One day Dizzy Dean's back brushed against the belt and his shirt and overalls were instantly grabbed. It spun him upside down, ripping off most of his clothes as he fought to keep himself from being dragged into the grinder's whirling flywheel. Dizzy was lucky to escape with no clothes and a lot of bruises.

The grinder, too, was a dangerous machine. Its large spinning blades could cut through anything, and at full speed it made a deafening roar. As bundles moved down the conveyor belt molasses was drizzled onto the corn from a 55-gallon drum. The ground-up corn stalks and molasses mixture was blown up a six-inch pipe that led to the top of the silo. Inside, six-foot sections of pipe bolted together sent the silage down to the slowly rising surface. As the level inside the silo rose, a section was removed and carried down the outside ladder.

It took four people to handle the job of packing down the silage. First, there was the person who guided the down-tubes, a tricky job because of the weight of the silage, and the need to aim the heavy tube exactly right. George's older brother, Whimpy, usually worked the tube. Another painted the walls with linseed oil (to keep the silage from sticking), traveling in an endless circle coating the walls with a wide brush. The other two stomped down the silage, packing it as tightly as possible to prevent air pockets that could reduce the storage volume and cause rot.

It was amazingly hot inside the silo, and we were all covered with silage, glued to us with sweat and molasses. It was also noisy, the sound of the grinder traveled straight through the metal tubes. Between wagon loads we flopped down on the bed of silage to catch our breath, then jumped back to work when the next batch came roaring in.

I'll admit it doesn't sound like a world of fun, but somehow it was. Again, it was real work, we did it as a team, and it felt good to be able to keep up and do a good job.

Other than Dizzy's near-miss, we only had one mishap I can recall, and it almost cost George his leg. When we stomped, we tried to stay close to the spray of silage coming out of the tube. Sometimes we got too close and the stuff hit our legs; no big deal, but it could bury your foot and slow you down. A large monkey wrench fell unnoticed off a wagon onto the conveyor belt. When it went into the grinder, the blades chewed it into dozens of metal chunks and sent them flying up the tube. In the silo it sounded like an explosion, the tube shook violently, and hunks of metal shot out the end just inches from George's leg. Whimpy managed to hold onto the tube and point it away from us. The blast only lasted a few seconds, but when it was over there were pieces of metal imbedded in the silo wall.

At lunch break, we went to Carlos and Mary's house. Mary was there most of the time since Grandmother was not in residence, and she always cooked an enormous meal. After we washed up and the blessing was said, we ate dinner, the major meal of the day. Virtually everything we ate was raised on the farm; even the soap was made in a big barrel in the wood shed.[15]

Dinner was truly a feast: salt-smoked ham, lamb, beef or venison, beans of every description, 'taters and 'maters, corn, peppers, home-baked biscuits and bread. There was no manners card in the middle of this table, and no one had to urge me to eat everything on my plate. After dinner we sat on the porch to rest and talk a while before going back to work.

Sometimes George and I climbed the apple tree in the front yard while the others talked. One day Carlos killed a copperhead in the woodshed, and before dinner he coiled it in a notch in the apple tree so you couldn't see it until you pulled up over the first big limb. I came out of that tree like a shot. We all laughed ourselves silly over it.

Unlike life under the Madam's nose, I was free to do what I wanted at Folly. Father wasn't there too much and Mother was usually busy with golf, bridge, or having tea with the Madam. When Father was around, he was more interested in golf than hanging around the farm. The fact I was up and out of the house in the morning and gone for the entire day didn't seem to either phase or interest them.

Exactly how I spent my time was never more than passing interest. What did catch their attention, what did rile them, however, was any talk about the people on the farm. It was fine to say I had hauled hay shocks or gone fishing with George, but I stayed well away from anything more than passing reference to the Bryants and Cleeks.

My parents assumed I ate "lunch" prepared by our cook. They would rather see me in a soup kitchen than eating at the Bryant's house. The reason was 70% snobbery and 30% fear of my being exposed to what they assumed to be unhygienic circumstances. In their minds, being of limited means automatically translated into being both ignorant of how to vote, and indifferent to cleanliness. The fact I had gotten a disease truly associated with being dirty at Calumet, but enjoyed perfect health in spite of repeated exposure to lowly farmers, didn't register with them.

There was one gap in my work, however, a wretched three-day self-inflicted illness that in a curious way did me a favor.

When we had a lot of hay to put up in a short time, or corn to harvest and grind for silage, extra men were brought in. Sometimes it was June Cleek, sometimes Dizzy Dean. In my short life I had never met a man like Dizzy Dean. Short, wiry and seemingly ill-tempered, he was utterly unable to string more than four or five words together without a cuss word. He chewed tobacco non-stop, spat, and cussed his way through the day. Tobacco juice stained his chin, and dripped onto his overalls.

But in spite of all the noise and tobacco juice, there was something fascinating and amazingly likable about Dizzy. Beyond an occasional "damn," no one else on Folly swore at all, yet they all accepted Dizzy just as he was. That's simply the way the man is; sort of like not noticing someone's limp or foreign accent.

Dizzy spoke the mountain language I loved so much, and in spite of the cussing, he was a great storyteller. Tales came non-stop, one after another, each more fantastic than the one before. My absolute favorite, though, was the one about how he and his twin brother, Dugan, killed a bobcat with their bare hands.

"That #!*! son of a bitch #!*!! cat prit' near#*!! tore my #*!!* arm off 'fore me an' Dugan #*!!* kilt that #!!* cat." Dizzy and Dugan are now in their eighties, and I went to see them to find out if the story as I remember it was actually true. What started as a simple visit with the brothers opened another window on life in Bath in the first half of the 20th century.

Dizzy's favorite chewing tobacco was a square plug about the size of half a Graham cracker, and twice as thick. Just about everyone chewed, but most used pouch tobacco. The advantage of a pouch was being able to take a partially-chewed "chaw," as it was known, out of one's mouth to "rest it" in the pouch with the unused tobacco. I remember someone asking if he could "beg a chaw" from a friend's pouch. The friend said yes, he could, but as he handed him the pouch he cautioned, "Watch it, I got a hot one in there."

For some wacky reason, I got it in my stupid head that I should try some chewing tobacco, too. So the next time we were in town and I had fifteen cents, I bought a plug of Yellow Mule at Morris' Dry Goods store. Not wanting anyone to see me chewing, I went down to the river, cut off a quarter of the plug with my pen knife just like Dizzy did, and popped it in my mouth.

It was here that I made my big mistake. Instead of giving it a chew and parking it 'twixt the gum and the cheek, I gave it a mighty bite and swallowed it. You can guess the rest. In about three minutes I became dizzy and nauseous. I knew I was in big trouble. I threw down the rest of the plug, and raced up the hill to the house. I threw up at the back door, and again and again in the bathroom. My parents were away, and Addie and Cora, the maids, took care of me. They put me on a bed on the sleeping porch since it had a wood floor and was easy to clean up.

I lay there for three days, spinning and unable to hold anything down. Addie and Cora gave me bottle after bottle of forbidden Coke, and finally I was able to stand up without feeling like I was on a Ferris wheel. Since then, I have never touched tobacco. And I hate all carnival rides, or anything else that travels in a fast circle.

Thanks, Dizzy, it was a tough way to learn, but that Yellow Mule sure did the trick.

Dizzy and Dugan were born Roy and Troy. Dugan recently told me they got their nicknames when they were about 13 because whenever someone called one boy, they both answered. Dizzy was named after a famous pitcher, Dugan has no idea where his name came from.

The boys were born in 1918. Their parents were forced to leave their home in Wise County, deeper in Appalachia, when the price of coal collapsed at the end of WWI, putting Mr. Dean out of work. He then found work stacking timber at the Tidewater Hardwood factory, and moved his family of fourteen to Bacova in 1926. Even though they lived in the company town, life was hard.

"We was barely makin' it. We hoed corn for a dime a day, but when the Depression come on us, we 'bout starved." The boys quit school and spent all of their time trapping for furs, and hunting and fishing for food. The deer herds were quickly decimated, as were all other easy-to-catch game like rabbits and squirrels. Fish were quickly cleaned out of the rivers. Even big snapping turtles disappeared.

Mink pelts still fetched a good price, but they weren't plentiful. Muskrat, possum and raccoon pelts were in demand, but lacking money to buy ammunition or fancy traps, the boys relied on snares and home-made Hoover traps.[16]

One of the most important sources of meat for the Dean family was the groundhog, or "whistle pig," as it was called.[17] "We'd spend all the #*! day diggin' them #%&*!* pigs." The boys took a shovel, a mattock, their favorite coon dog, Troubles, and went looking for groundhog holes. It usually took from one to three hours to dig out a groundhog. Usually the "pig" would go to the lowest part of his warren; occasionally, one would make a break for it. "Son of a bitch wouldn't get ten feet 'fore Troubles had him."

Troubles went everywhere with the boys. Dugan says the dog hunted so hard he would collapse at the end of the day. "Many a day I carried ol' Troubles home over my shoulder," Dugan says wistfully as he remembers his old pal.

"Me and Diz wouldn't a-took a thousand dollars for ol' Troubles." In fact, it was "ol' Troubles" who got Dizzy and Dugan into the fight with the bobcat. It seems the boys and their father were cutting firewood one afternoon when Troubles "winded" the cat, swam the river, and took off up the mountain. By the time the Deans caught up, Troubles had the cat treed in a big pine tree. They couldn't see the critter hidden in the upper part of the tree, and assumed it was a raccoon. Their only weapon was a pole ax, so they decided to cut the tree down to get the 'coon.

"The tree come down, an' a-fore you know'd it, the #*!&# cat jumped out of the tree on ol' Troubles. Me an' Diz looked at each other an' know'd we couldn't let that #%@&* cat kill ol' Troubles— we wouldn't a-took a thousand dollars for that dog. So I grabbed the son of a bitch by the back legs, and Diz grabbed the ^$%#@ cat by the front legs, and we stretched him out. The son of a bitch bit down on Diz's hand and wouldn't let go, and Paw kilt him with the pole ax."

The dog survived, Diz was okay ("weren't nothin' but a bite"), and they took the cat home. "He was a big son of a bitch, too. Had his legs over my shoulder and his $#%@@^ head was a-draggin' the ground."

They skinned the cat and sold the pelt for a pretty penny.

Later, in February of 1945, at the age of 26, Dugan got in big trouble when he shot and killed 17-year-old Aubrey Ryder. "We was drinkin' and arguin', and he just got his self kilt is all it was," Dugan told me. The article about the shooting in the local paper was bit more dramatic, saying Dugan shot Ryder:

> ...in a jealous rage over attention of a 7th grade school girl, pumped two slugs from a .38 revolver into the slight 17-year-old youth's body at arm length range.

The paper went on to say that Dugan told a witness before the shooting:

"This may be the last time I'll ever see you. Something's going to happen tonight."

Dugan served six-plus years of a 20-year sentence. While he was in prison, Dizzy married Aubrey Ryder's friend, Dorothy Kelley.

When Dugan was released he married, and the two brothers and their families have been close ever since. I recently asked Dorothy how they all managed to cope with such a difficult and conflicted situation.

"It was hard. Real hard," she said. She paused, looked at Dizzy with obvious affection and said, "But you have to move on."

Both Dizzy and Dugan are now in their eighties, still happily married and living only a few miles apart. The last time I saw Dizzy he was on his way out to hunt mushrooms. Dorothy packed a pouch with some lunch and a drink, and Dizzy left with a friend to spend the day on the mountain not too far from where he, Dugan, their father, and ol' Troubles killed the bobcat 75 years before.

One more note about Dugan. He's missing the fifth finger on his left hand, something I hadn't noticed until recently. I asked him how it happened.

"Weren't nothin'," he said rubbing his hand. "Diz was shootin' one day, and put up the pistol still loaded. I picked it up, an' was foolin' with it, an' the son of a bitch went off. Damn finger was hanging off flappin' around, so I walked down to Community House [our hospital, a five-mile walk for Dugan] and the doctor come in an' said he couldn't do nothin' so he snipped the bastard off, an' sewed it up."

"What did you do then?" I asked.

"I got a bottle, got drunk and said screw it. Weren't nothin'."

Dizzy showed me the scar on his hand where the bobcat bit him. The scar has faded over the years, but not the memory.

Dizzy told me something about my Uncle Jack I didn't know, but thinking about it, I might have guessed. The story fits Jack exactly as I remember him.

For many area residents, particularly for those who didn't own land or have well-fixed jobs at the Homestead, the Depression persisted well beyond WWII. As mentioned, fish and game, especially deer, were all but wiped out during the Depression, and poaching what little game was left was widespread. My grandparents were particularly sensitive about poachers. Because Grandfather was raising trout at the far end of the farm (where Glenn Williams and I later had our "hunt club"), he built a house there and installed a family to watch over his precious fish. They absolutely prohibited hunting anywhere on their property, and it became one of the few places in the county where deer were making a steady, highly protected, comeback.

Grandfather often broke the no-fishing rule, especially with the servants and with me. But Grandmother was unrelenting. She proudly told the story of the day Sam Snead showed up with a gift: a set of Patty Berg golf clubs. It was during WWII and a set of golf clubs was an impossible luxury. The Madam accepted the clubs. Sam was an avid fisherman, and as he was leaving he turned and said:

"Oh, by the way, I have my fishing rod in the trunk. Mind if I go down to the river for a little fishin' while I'm here?"

"You may not! You know the rule, Sam: no fishing. But thanks for the clubs."

Dizzy told me, somewhat apologetically, that before the house went up to guard the trout, he and Dugan (and probably others) often poached deer at that end of the farm. They raised the windshield on their truck and made a lightning midnight dash through a secret hole in the fence, racing down the mile-long meadow looking for grazing deer in their headlights. One quick shot and several week's worth of food was on the way back through the fence.

"We didn't do it for no fun," he said. "We done it 'cause we was hungry. And weren't none of it wasted, neither."

Then he told me about what Uncle Jack did. If at some point during hunting season the Madam left the farm, Jack made a few phone calls, and within an hour 20-30 people gathered at the barns. The group divided in two, one-half spreading into the woods near the barns, the other half entering the same woods two miles away along a back road. The two lines spread out over half a mile facing each other and the drive began, the two lines moving toward each other trapping the deer between. It sounds dangerous, but everyone knew those woods from years of either working on the place, or poaching, and no one let off a shot that didn't instantly bring down a deer.

The whole thing took about four hours start to finish. The deer were gutted, thrown into pickups or car boots (Dizzy's word, an interesting use of the English word for trunk), and everyone scattered. No trace of the hunt was left behind. When the Madam returned she had no idea Jack had master-minded a food bank that would easily serve one hundred people.

Another unforgettable character I met that summer was a blacksmith and skinner (mule driver) named Colonel Eskins. He was a tall, heavy-set man with a tobacco-stained white beard. He always wore a tan long-sleeved shirt, tan jodhpurs held up by wide suspenders, and a pair of "sixteens:" tall leather boots laced to his knees. His boots served a double purpose. The barns were overrun with cats, something that seemed particularly irksome to the Colonel. When he caught a male cat, he would stuff it head-first into a boot, lace it up tight so only the back end of the cat stuck out—then castrate the critter.

Colonel Eskins prided himself on being the "best goddam skinner in this-here place," and I never met anyone who disagreed. Many times I watched the Colonel arrive for work walking behind his two mules, guiding them with "gee" and "haw", their four long traces held loosely in this hands. Now that was something to see. He could back them anywhere, pull logs out of the woods weaving between trees, or work a hay rake all day rolling perfect win'rows. The only time he ever lost control of his team happened on Meadow Lane, on a steep hill near a cliff above the river. They were raking hay when they ran over a large nest of yellow jackets.

"Them #@^&* bees was all over us, an' the mules headed for the river—right over the goddam cliff." They tumbled down the cliff into the water, "tore the goddam rake all to hell," but the Colonel and the mules weren't seriously hurt. Whit Bogan, the carpenter on Meadow Lane for many years, confirmed the story, and said it only took the Colonel a week of blacksmith work to fix the rake. I wasn't the only one in awe of the man.

And, boy, could he tell a tall tale. At lunch we'd sit around, and to get him cranked up, someone would say he heard that old so-and-so had a great mule team, maybe even better than the Colonel's. That would get him started, for sure.

My favorite story is the one about the five-hundred-pound woman. Before the days of the tractor, traveling fairs featured "pulls" done with teams of horses and mules. There was one fair, according to the Colonel, that added a special challenge. A hole about six or seven feet deep was dug and a heavy log was set across the middle of the hole, held in place by large stakes driven into the ground. A stout rope was dangled into the hole, and around the waist of a five-hundred-pound woman; the other end was attached to a pair of mules. The woman would lean her back against the side of the hole closest to the mules, her feet braced against the other side. At the signal, the slack was taken up and the mules tried to pull the woman out of the hole.

No one could do it. Jammed into the hole with the rope cinched around that big log, she held on against all comers.

That is, until the Colonel hitched up his team. "Didn't take no time at all," he said. "Prit' soon she commenced to spittin' blood and screaming: 'Give him the money!! Give him the money!!'"

On Saturday nights the Bryants and the Cleeks often went to a friend's place for a square dance. I only got to go twice, but I remember both as if they were yesterday. We rode down the gorge in the back of Carlos' truck and when we got to the McClintic place, the men moved every stick of furniture, except stiff-back chairs, out into the yard. The chairs were placed around the perimeter of the front rooms, and in the kitchen. While the men moved the furniture, the women laid out a huge meal. June Cleek called dances, and the music was usually a guitar and a fiddle, sometimes a banjo.

The fiddle player was Whit Bogan. Whit didn't quite clear five feet, but he could swing a hammer so accurately he wouldn't leave a dimple in the wood when he drove a nail. When he played the fiddle, his shoulders dipped and his rhythm foot bounced up to the level of his chin. He grinned the whole time he was playing, as if he were the happiest man in the country.

He was also the best pistol shot around. He drove an old Ford pick-up and carried a nine-shot H&R .22 pistol under the seat. When he spotted a groundhog, you'd see the gun barrel slide out of the window, but from the front, all you could see of Whit was the top of his head. And he didn't miss.

Whit's wife, Beulah, was over six feet tall, but in spite of the dramatic difference in their heights, I never heard anyone joke or even remark about it. Quite the opposite: they were regarded as a perfect match, and Whit was fiercely protective of Beulah, though to look at them you'd think it was the other way around. They had four daughters, all of whom grew up to be talented musicians.

In spite of his size, Whit was strong as a mule. One time when they lived in a fairly remote cabin on Back Creek, two cousins celebrating the release of one of the boys from the county jail, stumbled on the cabin and asked to come in for some food. I'll call them Johnny and Bob since one of them is still alive and I don't want to embarrass him.

175

Whit Bogan (with two of his daughters) playing at a square dance at Jack Williams' cabin. Dancers do the dos-a-dos. (Photograph courtesy of Dr. Jack Williams).

They were both roaring drunk. Whit was sitting in his easy chair, and apparently Bob made the mistake of looking down at Whit and saying how good Beulah looked to a man who'd been in the pokey for the past six months. Whit balled up his fist, shot straight up out of the chair and clocked the boy on the chin, breaking his jaw and knocking him stone-cold out. He and Beulah dragged Bob out on the porch, pushed Johnny out the door, and bolted it. Johnny somehow dragged his brother back to the truck, and by morning they were gone.

The guitar player was Nelson Carpenter, the town barber, and resident expert on just about everything going on in the county. Like Whit, he always wore a good-natured grin, and could play and carry on a couple of conversations at the same time.

Before the meal started someone said a prayer of thanks, then everybody filed through the kitchen to get their plate filled. After eating, June took a few minutes to make sure everyone—especially the kids—knew the calls. I felt terribly awkward at first, but no one seemed to mind if I started in the wrong direction in a dos-a-dos or a promenade. By the end of the evening I had the basics, and after that never missed a chance to go to a square dance.

During the evening there would be a cakewalk or two. Everyone put a few coins in the hat, the band played, and we stepped two-by-two past the caller until the music suddenly stopped. The couple in front of the caller won the cake. The little bit of money collected went to the musicians and the caller.

At the end of the evening the furniture was replaced, hampers were repacked, and at ten-thirty or so I hopped out of Carlos' truck in front of my house and said good night. My parents were always out late on Saturday night, and the staff usually had the night off. I went to bed tired and happy.

Unfortunately, in that same summer my parents decided I was old enough to go with them to the Homestead to dance. By contrast, these were awful evenings for me. First, I had to dress up—

it was a white coat for the men, gowns for the ladies. I drank ginger ale and prayed I wouldn't have to dance with my grandmother. She smelled funny and my arms weren't long enough to keep my face out of her giant breasts.

When Mary was away, her mother, Granny Cleek, came down to fix the mid-day dinner at the Bryant's. She was slightly built—just short of fragile looking—and her shoulders were rounded from both osteoporosis and years of hard work. In 1941, her husband, Floyd Cleek, was struck by a branch that fell out of a chestnut tree he was chopping down. He survived the accident, but "he wasn't right after that," and died a year later at the age of 76.

June showed me the spot where his father was injured, and while we stood looking at the grove of trees he told me a little about his father. He was a farmer, and like his father before him, an expert butcher. Before there were reliable trucks to haul livestock to market—around the time of WWI—the Cleeks drove their cattle and sheep on foot over fifty miles to the market in Marlinton, West Virginia. Along the way they camped in the woods or stayed in a friend's barn. It was what one did to make a living, simple as that.

Granny lived up at the end of the road with June and rarely left the hollow. She always wore a bonnet and skirt, and while warm and friendly, she seemed reserved, cautious, even a bit timid. She, too, spoke the mountain language, and I loved to listen to her talk when we sat on the porch at the Bryant's after dinner.

One day, out of nowhere, she said I ought to come up and visit her, "set a spell," as she put it. I was nine, and having an adult notice me enough to want my company was, to me, a serious invitation. The first time my parents were out, and I wasn't working, I started up the hollow. It was a long and magical walk, even scary at first, especially in the narrowest part of the hollow. It was one thing to ride up the road in Carlos' pickup, but walking gave it a whole new feel. The trees seemed bigger, the rock wall taller, and all the shadows longer and more suggestive when seen in slow motion.

There were also sounds to be sorted out. The crows seemed more alarmed than usual and the breeze caused branches to scrape and groan. Carlos had killed a rattlesnake where a spring overflowed into the road at the bend below the Ailstock's house. I picked my way around that spot very carefully. I didn't know James Ailstock's family so I just walked by on that first walk to Granny's. After the Ailstock's, the hollow opened up somewhat and even the graveyard up on the hill didn't seem too scary.

Finally I rounded the fence into Granny Cleek's yard. She seemed genuinely happy to see me, something I really couldn't figure out; after all, I was just a skinny kid who could barely lift a bucket of milk. But she welcomed me and I fell in step as she did her chores. We weeded the garden, hauled water, fed the stock, and when she cooked I peeled apples and potatoes, or dumped grease in the soap barrel.

And we talked. I guess I was full of questions about how everything worked, what it was like in the old days in the late 1800's, before automobiles and tractors. The Cleek family had lived in that hollow for six generations. They were living there before the first Hirsh left Germany for the States in the early 1800's. While it seemed remote and isolated to me, it was the opposite to Granny. One family lived over that ridge, another past that hollow, and two more over the near hill. The families all helped each other out with farming, they all socialized and went to church together.

Typically, each family owned one piece of farming equipment, and by sharing they could grow and harvest just about anything. If one family's land was best suited for oats and another for corn, that's the way each was planted. At the end of the season the crops were divided up so everyone had what was needed.

There was a one-room schoolhouse in the hollow. Grades 1-8 were taught by two women from Warm Springs who rotated the job every week. Before the automobile became available and reliable enough to make it up the hollow, every Monday one of the teachers would ride or walk from Warm Springs about ten miles away, stay with one of the families in the hollow, and leave on Friday afternoon.

When you look at it from Granny's perspective, she lived in a settled, supportive community where they had just about everything they needed. No frills, mind you, but no one had the least notion of missing anything important.

The REA brought in electricity in 1945. Before that, no one in the hollow needed a light bulb; hot water was boiled on the wood stove. Lack of refrigeration, incidentally, was not a problem. A lot of the meat, especially bacon and ham, was salted and smoked; the rest—like chicken—was eaten fresh. Wild meat was dried or canned. In the summer, butter, eggs and milk were kept in a cave in the hill above the cabin. The temperature was always below 55 degrees, and shelf space was never an issue.

For a long time after the introduction of radio no one in the hollow had such a device. I always assumed that radios arrived with electricity just after WWII. But quite recently, behind an old chest at Granny's place, a battery-operated Sears & Roebuck radio was found. It's a Silvertone Neutrodyne, a beautiful wooden box containing large vacuum tubes and an ancient paper speaker. Large alligator clips connected to a battery powered it. The hollow wasn't as isolated as one might think.

Even the Great Depression didn't bring as much hardship to the hollow as elsewhere. People were largely self-sufficient, no one had a big bank loan, and folks continued to barter with each other and at the local store for basics. Times were hard for everyone, and it was relatively easy to forgo what few luxuries people might have had before the Depression began.

The Homestead was full the day before the crash in October, 1929. The next day the C&O railroad brought 6 extra cars into Hot Springs, and in a few days there were only a handful of guests left.

But over the next year the great old Hotel recovered, guests returned, and commerce with the local community revived. Farmers sold livestock and produce to the Hotel, or—like Floyd Cleek—provided a special service for cash.

My parents had it wrong. The folks living up the road they never traveled were not backward, disconnected relics scraping a living out of whatever we were kind enough to send their way. Far from it, they were a durable, patient and cohesive people with roots as deep or deeper than any of ours, and a value system that in many instances made ours look shabby.

Many times when I asked a question about our ancestry, or something personal, such as why everyone seemed so ready to dump on Uncle Jack, Father would draw back in a defensive, angry way, and either avoid the question, or snarl at me to mind my own business.

It took years for me to uncover my family's heritage. Granny Cleek explained hers in a few short visits.

When I left Granny's, she always gave me a biscuit smeared with churned butter and a piece of home-cured ham. The biscuit didn't last a quarter of a mile but made me so thirsty I had to take my chances with the rattlesnakes at the spring on the way back down the hollow.

I walked up to Granny's at least half a dozen times at the end of that summer and got to know the rocks and shadows as friendly companions. I met James Ailstock's wife, Edna, and when she was home I stopped to bum a glass of water, sit on her porch and chat. Like so many of the folks in Bath, she was musical and played a guitar. Sometimes she sang hymns for me, songs I already knew from Uncle Gene.

A week or so after Labor Day it was time to go back to Montclair to start the new school year. I made one last sad hike up the hollow to say goodbye to Granny and June. We sat on the front porch and talked, and just before I was about to leave Granny asked me, "Philip, when you grow up, what are you going to do?"

She was dead serious, and I was on the spot. This was no time to say I didn't know, or give some quick, disingenuous answer. I was almost ten, and at that point in my life I don't think I had given it much thought. In some vague way I knew I was expected to go into the engineering business, whatever that was. I also knew that meant working with Father—not an appealing idea.

I knew Granny expected an answer with heft, and once said, it would be like a promise. "A doctor," I said after a long pause. "Yes, Granny, I want to be a doctor."

As I said it, a dark look clouded her face. She suddenly looked sad, and far away. I felt I had said something terribly wrong, but I couldn't understand what it was.

The moment passed, I said goodbye, and she gave me a long hug and a biscuit. I waved as I turned onto the road at the fence and started back down the hollow. I hoped I was far enough away so she couldn't see my tears. That was the longest and most miserable walk I had ever taken. What had I said that upset her so? And more to the point, what could I do to make it up to her? But it would be until the next spring before I could see her again. I had a long time to think about it.

In fact, I didn't see her again until the following summer, and because we were back at Meadow Lane, I lost most of my contact with Folly Farm, the Bryants and the Cleeks. No Saturday night square dances, hauling hay shocks or long walks up to Granny's. I did get to stomp some silage at Meadow Lane, but it wasn't the same. I didn't go into the fields, and when I rode it was on Little Oscar. Heels down. Back straight. Hold your reins up.

God! I missed Petunia and Begonia.

When I finally got to see Granny she was bright and cheerful, no sign of the gloom I had brought to her the previous fall. I don't remember how many times I saw her that summer, probably not more than two or three, and only for short visits. No time to do chores or really talk. But she always gave me a ham biscuit when I left. At least there was that.

Over the next several summers I saw her infrequently. When I was fifteen I had my driver's license, a car, and a summer job with the company in New Jersey. At the end of the summer I drove down to Virginia before going off to prep school. Just before I left, I visited Granny.

We sat on the porch just like always and talked about this and that. She seemed older and a little tired, or maybe it was just me, I don't know. But in the middle of our chat she asked me the question I dreaded. "Are you still plannin' on bein' a doctor?" She had the same serious look on her face I remembered from five years before.

This was no time to weasel out. "Yes, Granny, I am."

She sighed, nodded her head a bit and said, "Well... better come with me, then."

I followed her into the wide front hallway with a wood stove in the middle that served as a parlor. On the right, just inside the front door, there was a door I had never seen open. It always seemed like the room behind it didn't exist, and I often wondered what was on the other side of that door.

Granny took a key out of her apron—one of those old-timey, long-shaft skeleton keys with a little square cut-out on the end—and unlocked the door. The room was dark, and I could only make out shapes, but it seemed completely filled with furniture and random stacks of stored items. A strong musty odor hung in the gloomy stillness of the room.

Granny pulled back a dusty curtain to let a little light in. Even so, it took a minute for my eyes to adjust to the darkness.

It was a good-sized room, maybe ten by twelve. There was a fireplace blocked by a steamer trunk, an old pianoforte against one wall, and a pump organ across from it on the opposite wall. In the middle there was a narrow bed piled high with clothing; boxes and lop-sided stacks of books crowded the rest of the room. I stood by the door while Granny moved through piles of books looking for something.

Finally she found it, and without saying a word, she locked the door, put the key back in her apron and led the way back outside to the porch. I squinted in the bright light and tasted the freshness of the air as we sat down. Granny held a small, thick book in her lap. It had a black soft cover and looked like it might be a Bible.

We sat in silence for what felt like an eternity. Granny stared at the book, her face sad as if the book was whispering something painful. I tried to look away, feeling like my eyes were intruders blundering rudely into the exquisite privacy of those moments.

Then she looked up, her face seemed to clear, and the slightest smile appeared. "Here," she said handing me the book, "If you're going to be a doctor, you'll need this."

I was holding **Gould's Medical Dictionary**, 1928 edition. "40,000 Medical Words Pronounced and Defined." On the title page it was signed:

> *Dorothy Cleek*
> *C&O Hospital*
> *Clifton Forge, Va.*

Under the title, in the same hand, the ink yellowed with age:

> *To thine own self be true*
> *& it must follow as night*
> *the day & how can'ts thou*
> *be false to any man.*

I had no idea who Dorothy Cleek was. Granny explained that Dorothy was her daughter and Mary Bryant's twin sister. She

Dorothy L. Cleek in Chicago, 1932.
(Photograph courtesy of Mr. June Cleek).

graduated from the C&O Nursing School in June, 1931. Shortly after starting work as a nurse, she fell and injured her hip. An examination revealed she had Pott's disease—tuberculosis of the backbone. She returned home and in May, 1937, after five years of pain and illness, died in the mysterious room off the parlor. After the funeral, Granny put all of Dorothy's possessions in the room and locked the door.

Granny talked a little about Dorothy—she called her Dot—and later I learned more about her from her brother, June. Of her three children, she was the only one who went past the eighth grade.

Dorothy wanted to go on to high school, a formidable undertaking in the late 1920's. There were only two high schools in the county, and if you wanted a high school education, you had to find your way to the county road to be picked up by the school bus. For Dorothy, that meant a four-mile hike on a logging trail up a steep mountain, and down the other side to the road. The entire family made the round trip every Sunday for worship at the Eden Church. Standing on the knoll above the house with June recently, he shook his head as he recalled his sister Dorothy's determination, and described the awful winter weather she had to get through to attend Valley High.

But she made it through four years of high school, was graduated with honors, and enrolled in the C&O Hospital nursing school in Clifton Forge, about thirty miles from home. She was graduated in 1931—again with honors. She went to Chicago to work, but shortly after she started she became ill and returned home. There was no treatment for tuberculosis in the 1930's, and no way to arrest its slow, painful inevitability. Shortly before she died, her twin sister Mary had her first child, named Carlos after his father.

"Why, he's a regular Whimpy," Dorothy said when she first saw him. It was not an insult or a put-down as we might think of the word today. Little Carlos was a robust baby, perhaps a bit chubby like the popular 1929 Popeye cartoon character, J. W. Wimpy, who ate hamburgers by the stack.

I couldn't just drive off and not return after the emotion of that afternoon. I went back for one more visit before heading north. We talked more about Dorothy and I asked about the piano and organ in her room. She was always interested in music, Granny said, and learned to play by staying after church to practice on the organ. The minister's wife gave her lessons and she often returned home after dark on Sunday evening.

I asked Granny if the organ still worked. She didn't know, but we went back into the room, cleared a space for the stool and I tried pumping the two foot pedals. It was an old Kimbal "parlor organ" sold by the thousands in the early part of the last century. In the days before electricity and radio, pump organs were immensely popular. Sacred songs were played as much as old standards, and families spent hours listening and singing together.

One of the foot pedals worked but the other was stuck, so I got on the floor, and using a candle saw that mice had eaten the leather strap connecting the pedal to the bellows. I took off my belt and found it was a perfect fit and in a few minutes I was able to play.

For no reason other than I liked the song, I played The Old Rugged Cross. When I finished, I stood up and turned around. Granny was standing right behind me, tears flowing down her cheeks. Once again, a dreadful sinking sensation swept over me.

"Granny!" I said. "What have I done?"

It took her a minute, she sort of smiled through the tears and said, "The last time that organ was played was at Dot's funeral. And the last song played on it was her favorite—The Old Rugged Cross."

When I left that day I knew there was to be no retreat from the commitment made to Granny. I seldom saw Granny after that, summer jobs and school made it increasingly hard to spend any time

Granny Cleek, her husband Floyd, son June Cleek, and grandchildren
George (left) and Whimpy (right) taken in 1939.
The shuttered windows of Dorothy's room are seen in the background.
(Photogragh courtesy of Mr. George Bryant).

in Bath. But we kept up with each other, and when I was graduated from medical school in 1964, I received a card of congratulations. It was signed:

> *Your friend,*
> *Emma Cleek*

Granny died in December, 1965.

The dictionary has always been with me. It's sitting on the shelf in front of me now. I often pick it up, scan the pages, and feel the softness of its cover. Once in a while I find an underline or a note I hadn't seen before. Each time it's like finding a little treasure, and I think I hear the whisper too.

Chapter X

Moonshine

No story about long dark hollows in Appalachia would be complete without mention of moonshine, perhaps the only piece of regional history where the gap between myth and reality is pretty narrow. There really were stills in operation throughout Appalachia during Prohibition, and the people who ran them were a tough, no-nonsense crowd. It was often a violent enterprise, and the government spent a lot of time and money trying to disrupt the industry. Quite a few—on both sides—lost their lives.

Not only did terrain and local resentment of federal government authority make enforcement difficult and dangerous, but there was no one moonshine "mob" or unified criminal command to fight. Moonshiners were loners, a few mountain men operating moveable stills under cover of darkness, miles from a highway, protected by a friendly network of family and friends. The product itself was easily hidden, and when distributed in small amounts, virtually impossible to track.

The main point of vulnerability was on the highway when larger quantities were moved to cities like Washington, D.C. Even then, bootleggers were tough to catch because ingenious mechanics created all sorts of innocent-looking specialized vehicles to move large volumes of moonshine. When a bust was made it usually meant intercepting the shipment, and only the driver went down. Drivers were well paid, and usually had no idea who made the whiskey or where it was distilled, so an arrest netted the government nothing more than a car and someone to lock up for six months. For the driver, it was an inconvenience. If he kept his mouth shut, he had a job and back pay coming when he got out.

Making whiskey was an American tradition begun well before the Revolutionary War. It wasn't illegal then; indeed, it was an entirely normal and respectable undertaking done right out in the open. Coins and printed money were a rarity until the early 19th century. Folks traded what they made and grew for what they needed. Small amounts of homemade whiskey were part of the barter system as much as anything else, and often paid as wages to itinerant preachers. There was no shame in making or using a little whiskey. Alcoholism was another story; that was considered a sin. But the quantities available were so small—at least in the beginning—that it was a self-limiting problem.

Making whiskey went underground in the late 18th century when George Washington's Secretary of the Treasury, Alexander Hamilton, got congress to levy a tax on distilled spirits as a way to raise money to pay the country's enormous debt. A large portion of the nation's spirits came from about 1,200 distillers in western Pennsylvania, and they weren't about to pay an excise tax on their product. The Whiskey Rebellion, as it came to be known, came to a head in 1794 when 15,000 Federal troops were called out to crush the uprising and force compliance. The rebellion quickly fell apart, and the taxes were collected.

Around the time of the War of 1812, the distillers again rebelled, and no serious effort was made to enforce the tax until the early 1850's. By 1862 the matter was deemed severe enough to warrant a special division of government just to collect the 20 cents per gallon whiskey tax. The new department was called the Internal Revenue Service.

In 1876 the IRS estimated there were 3,000 illegal stills making 150,000 gallons a day. By 1894 the tax had risen to $1.10 a gallon. In 1918 Prohibition made all spirits illegal—tax or not—and bootlegging went from simply illegal to frankly dangerous.

The art of making quality whiskey arrived with the earliest settlers, and was well known throughout Appalachia. Grains and fruit—the raw material of whiskey—were abundant, and with a little patience and a good still, a high-quality product could be made. It had many well-recognized names like white lightning, stump liquor, moonshine, bootleg, and corn liquor.

Good moonshine is pure alcohol, contains no chemicals, and doesn't leave you with a hangover. The best 'shine is made from white corn which is husked, put in water until it sprouts, then dried, ground, and made into "corn malt." Corn meal (ground corn) is cut into hot water and cooked down to produce "mash." The mash is combined with the malt in hot water, and rye flour added which causes the mixture to "head," or foam. Then the alcohol is distilled off yielding a weakly alcoholic product called "singlings." It is then re-distilled producing "doublings." At that point it is "proofed" by shaking it enough to produce bubbles in a clear glass jar. The bubbles are then "read:" it is 100 proof (50% alcohol) when the bubbles bead half way up the jar. The final step is to pass it through a charcoal filter.

Making whiskey is a time consuming and labor intensive venture. During Prohibition sugar was used to accelerate the process by shortening the time needed to convert the cornstarch to sugar. Mountain bootleggers frowned on it, calling the resulting product rotgut, panther piss, and coffin varnish.

Stills were located deep in the hollows far from roads, peering eyes and sensitive noses. Moonshining is a smelly, water-hungry business. The creeks that flow down every hollow provided an endless supply of pure mountain water, and the woods yielded downed, dried hardwoods that burned without telltale smoke. The word " moonshine" implies that distilling was a nighttime activity. Stills were often started at night to minimize telltale smoke signals, but once the fires were burning the still ran for as long as a week to produce a good "run." The word "moonshine," incidentally, did not originate in Appalachia during the Depression; actually, it's an 18th century English word. At that time French cognac was heavily taxed, and brandy smugglers made the dash across the English Channel at night—under the light of the moon.

In the 1890's it cost about twenty cents to make a gallon of legitimate whiskey. In order to be sure the distillers were paying their tax, the federal government assigned a "gauger" to distilleries to test, tax, and stamp every barrel made. The minimum amount for a legal sale (called a "prescription") was five gallons. The gauger was paid $75 a month by the government, but his room and board were the responsibility of the distiller. If that wasn't bad enough, each producer was required to have a separate—and very expensive— distillery license.

None of this went over very well in fiercely independent and impoverished Appalachia, and the outlaw moonshiner was born. Prohibition just added more wood to the moonshiner's fire.

Bath County was a natural place for moonshine production. It was sparsely populated, isolated, had long remote hollows and an abundance of fresh water. Virtually every hollow has at least one good spring.

When Prohibition began, confiscation of illegal spirits was so common the sheriff dug a deep hole behind the jail and capped it with an iron grate to provide an easy and visible method to dispose of captured 'shine. As a kid Gene Folks watched his father pour barrels of the stuff down the drain, whiskey that was sometimes captured at considerable risk.

MY FATHER-1916- WAS SHERiff-for -27 YEARS

Sheriff Charles Gum on his horse, Pat.
(From the Gum family scrapbook donated to the Bath County Historical society by
Sheriff Gum's daughter, Mrs. Lucille Puffenbarger).

In 1923 Judge Stephenson decided to remove Sheriff Gum from office—"set him down" was the official term. I don't know just why, something between the two men. Gene recalled that Gum had a reputation as a lady's man, and didn't have the highest moral values. One contemporary newspaper reported a rumor that Gum and some local moonshiners had a whiskey deal that went sour. Whatever the reason, the judge asked Gene's father to serve out the last 2 years of Gum's term, and he accepted—reluctantly. During his brief time in office he tangled with a number of moonshiners including several members of the Messer family.

George Washington Messer, Sr., came from the Tug Fork of the Big Sandy River area along the West Virginia and Kentucky border, the place where the Hatfields and McCoys fought it out in the late 19th century. One of his clan, Aleck Messer, boasted he had killed 27 men before he was arrested and given a life sentence. One of his worst crimes was the murder of a group of McCoys, including a 12 year-old boy. "Devil" Anse Hatfield ("Six feet of Devil and 180 pounds of Hell") was blamed for the crime, but he always denied it, and it may well have been the work of Aleck Messer. Whatever the truth, the Messers were a rough crowd.

Incidentally, the exact relationship between George Washington, Sr., and Aleck is not clear. According to the *Covington Virginian*, December 9, 1929:

G.W. "probably didn't know exactly himself. That they were kin and of the same clan there is no doubt. Some say he was a younger brother; others a nephew; some a cousin; probably all three, for there was much inter-marrying and general co-mingling among the Tug River folk."

They were also heavily into making and using moonshine. During his term in office, Sheriff Folks had several run-ins with G.W., Sr., as well as his sons George Washington, Jr., Benton and Lafayette. Toward the end of his time in office, Sheriff Folks was approached by some "revenuers," as federal alcohol tax enforcers were known, who had information about a big still somewhere deep in Thacker's hollow. They wanted the sheriff and his deputies to guide a raid on the camp.

Unfortunately, as the group made its way up the steep and brushy hollow, they were ambushed—maybe by Messers, maybe by somebody else—it was never proven one way or the other. A revenuer was killed and the moonshiners got away. Shortly after, another election was held. Sheriff Folks refused to run, Charlie Gum was easily re-elected, and Gene's father happily went back to being a storekeeper.

But the Messer story wasn't over.

Sheriff Gum displays a captured still in 1926.
The "worm" can be seen on the hood of his truck in the background.
(Photograph courtesy of Mrs. Lucille Puffenbarger).

In the summer of 1929 Sheriff Gum arrested several Messers at Rhododendron Lodge, a popular grocery, dance hall, and drinking place on the east side of Warm Springs mountain. Decades earlier it had been a tavern and the place were the stagecoach stopped before going over Warm Springs mountain. During Prohibition it was a wild place, and one of the few venues where daring black musicians could earn money playing for white audiences. The *Bath County Enterprise* reported the Messers "were drinking and got into several fights and were arrested and given punishments by the magistrates trying the cases." The incident "caused Geo. W. Messer, Sr. and the young Messers to become revengeful toward anything taking place at Rhododendron Lodge."

The youngest Messer was sent to "the reformatory," and GW Sr. and Jr. went to the road gang. The *Lexington Gazette* reported that a "shooting affray" was inevitable between Gum and the Messers because GW Sr. sent a message to Gum after his release saying: "If you ever come after me, better bring the undertaker with you."

On the night of December 7, 1929, Sheriff Gum was again summoned to the Lodge to deal with the Messers. They were drunk, fighting—and armed. Sheriff Gum and his deputy arrived and confronted both George Washington Sr. and Jr. Shots were fired and Sheriff Gum was killed on the spot. The senior Messer was hit but managed to escape. No one wanted to go after the wounded Messer in the dark, but the next morning a posse found his body behind a log in the near-by woods.

George Washington Messer, Jr., was also shot, but he was captured, and recovered from his wounds. He was convicted of the murder of Sheriff Gum and given a 35-year sentence. He later developed TB and was released from prison. No one knows what happened to him after that.

Sheriffs and judges were elected or rejected largely based on their attitude toward the moonshiners. Of course the temperance crowd wanted still-busting crusaders. But most folks wanted just enough law enforcement to keep things from getting out of hand, but not enough to shut off the supply of whiskey completely.

My first exposure to moonshine—when I was about seven—came right out of *Thunder Road*. Just before breakfast one morning we heard sirens coming from the direction of the recently paved main road. They quickly grew louder, and it was obvious someone was coming up our lane fast. It's only a mile from the house to the road, but in seconds a car roared up the lane, past the house headed for the barns. Two police cars were right behind and going just as fast.

They all managed to round the barns without wrecking or killing anyone. The road runs another half mile and dead ends at the poultry coops. When the driver of the first car ran out of road, he braked, went into a slide and ended up in the middle of a huge turkey pen.

By the time we got there the cops had the driver in one of their cars, and the workers were running around trying to catch the turkeys. It was my first up-close look at a real criminal, and I must say it was disappointing. He didn't look anything like Robert Mitchum. He was short, wore a natty tweed coat, a tie, and a slouch hat. He looked totally indifferent—even bored—and waved to us as they drove him away.

The car's trunk and hood were both open. A large metal tank, obviously full of moonshine, took up the trunk. The men admired the special suspension and souped-up engine that gave the innocent-looking car its amazing power.

I didn't hear much about moonshine when I was young. I heard Father tell people he used to buy it over the line in West Virginia, and I'm sure the grooms and other workers used it, too, but no one talked about it—especially to a kid.

When I got to college some of my friends asked if I could get some white lightening when I was back in Virginia. I asked Ralph

Cleek, the man who ran the gristmill, where I might be able to buy some. Ralph suggested I get in touch with June Buzzard, again: just over the line in West Virginia.

Ralph warned me that there was a definite protocol involved in buying moonshine, and it might take me several visits before I was successful. There was also a good chance I wouldn't be able to buy any no matter how careful and respectful I was. That's just the nature of doing business with June Buzzard.

How right he was. That was the start of a relationship that only lasted a few years, but introduced me to one of the most colorful and unusual people I have ever known.

It took quite a while to locate June's place. He lived in a sparsely settled part of West Virginia, well off of the main road. All I knew was he lived "up a hollow" off a county road. Trouble is, there are a lot of hollows in Pocahontas County, all narrow and wooded, and many sported a trail or even a dirt road. It was impossible to see far enough up to see who—if anybody—lived up there. This was definitely not a place where strangers were welcome. Blundering uninvited up someone's road could get you shot, simple as that.

After two unsuccessful attempts to find June, I got Wayne, one of our farmers who knew June, to go with me, not only to find the place, but more importantly, to introduce me. He advised I take along a few things to trade, and cautioned me never to offer cash for anything. June considered himself an antique dealer, not a storekeeper. And having something old to trade was a whole lot better way to get started than walking in and asking for moonshine.

Wayne knew exactly where the hollow was. It was one I had passed a dozen times before. Like many others, it had a menacing hand-painted KEEP OUT sign nailed to a tree. We drove in a hundred yards or so, parked, I took out the few items I had brought to trade, and we started up the narrow road along a small creek. The steep sides of the hollow quickly closed in, and the temperature dropped precipitously. Huge pines towered over us, limiting the summer sun to long shafts of light like hundreds of spotlights aimed at random from the tops of the trees. As we approached his cabin, June's coon dogs sensed us and started howling. For sure, no one was going to sneak up on June Buzzard.

The trail ended in a small clearing. A cabin straddled the little creek on the far side of the open space, its sides nearly touching the walls of the hollow. On the right, there was a chicken coop, shed and a dog pen full of hounds all standing with their front feet on the wire barking at us. A couple of old cars and lot of ancient farm equipment crowded the rest of the clearing.

June stood at the door of the cabin eyeing us suspiciously, but recognizing Wayne, he smiled and came out. Introductions were made, then June and Wayne moved off to the shed to talk, leaving me standing in the middle of the clearing feeling foolishly conspicuous and way out of my league. Several children in the cabin eyed me cautiously, but stayed well away from the door. The dogs continued to howl.

I put my things in the bed of a rusted pick up, sat down on a log, and waited. Finally, the conference was over and June came and asked what I wanted to trade. I showed him the things I had brought, but he didn't seem interested. He asked what I wanted from him, and (previously coached by Wayne) I mentioned old guns and Ford truck parts. In fact, I had an old Ford truck and I did collect guns so I was genuinely interested in what he might have.

June said if I had any old guns to trade, he'd be interested. Quick as that, he turned and went back in the cabin and shut the door. Wayne and I retreated back to the car in silence. I was disappointed and felt foolish for involving Wayne in what was obviously a huge waste of time. Wayne disagreed, and told me June had taken him to the woodshed to find out who I was and what I wanted. Wayne told him straight out I wanted some corn liquor, but knew better than to ask until June could trust me. I was startled and more than a little embarrassed, but Wayne assured me I did just fine, and I would be wise to visit several more times before I brought up the subject of moonshine.

In essence, it was all part of the dance, and so far, in spite of my intense discomfort, I hadn't stepped on anyone's toes. I followed Wayne's advice and paid several visits to June, each time trading gun parts, and never even hinting any interest in alcohol.

All our transactions were done out in the yard in front of the cabin. He had things stashed all over the place: in the cabin, the shed, the chicken coop, and even the doghouse. As each item was brought out of its hiding place, June would say he just wanted to show it to me—it wasn't for trade—and then tell a long story about where it came from, how many people wanted it, and how reluctant he was to give it up. Everything was a precious favorite, no one ever had one just like it before, but, yes, he liked me and he might let it go, knowing how badly I wanted it. But first he had to "think on it."

Even though we were getting along just fine, I still felt anxious about bringing up the subject of whiskey. It really was fun to banter with June, and I hated to risk our evolving friendship over an ill-timed question about moonshine. But I was running out of gun parts and time, so I decided to up the ante a bit. I offered to trade an old Marlin rifle if June had a comparable priceless antique firearm.

That did it. I was invited into the cabin to see his "collection." I had never been closer than the front door, nor had I spoken directly to June's wife or any of his children. The door led into the kitchen area. I couldn't see much in the gloomy interior, and June didn't linger to introduce me to his family. I nodded hello, and followed June up some rickety steps to the loft, an open area hemmed in by the sloping roof. There was a small window over the stairs for light. The floor and walls of the loft were completely covered with guns, and countless pieces and parts of guns. Here and there I spotted a car part or a something I couldn't identify, but it was mostly pieces of guns. One couldn't step without first pushing something out of the way. We cleared a spot and squatted on the floor.

"Well," he said in a satisfied way, "Here it is. My collection." I mumbled something about it being pretty amazing, and he allowed as how that was so. "But that ain't all I got," he said with a laugh. He showed me one of a number of homemade articulated tin figures, cutouts of people and animals connected by metal strips loosely riveted so the two figures could be moved. The one he showed me was a silhouette of a naked man and a woman facing each other. When the figures were moved...well, you can imagine the rest.

We had a good laugh over it and a few others he had made, then we turned our attention to the collection. Like everything else June had, each piece had its own story, and once he started telling a tale, there was no way to deflect him. After quite a long time we settled on a trade (he clearly got the better part of that one), and started toward the stairs.

June went first, and after he had taken a few steps down, he turned back toward me. I was still crouched over to keep from banging my head on the rafters. Only the upper part of June's body was visible, silhouetted against the small, cobweb-clouded window. It was hard to make out his facial features, but he spoke with the utmost gravity:

"Philip, you seen my collection, and now you know what I got, so you can tell why it has me plum worriet." I had no idea where he was going with this, but I knew it was important, so I said something vague like, "Well, I reckon."

"Yep, you know, sometimes I can't sleep just thinkin' about it. What if someone was to sneak up here in the middle of some night, hit me up side of my head, kill me, and steal my guns?!"

He shook his head in a slow, troubled way. "Next day, Philip, next day the newspapers all over the country would say: Who Killed June Buzzard?!"

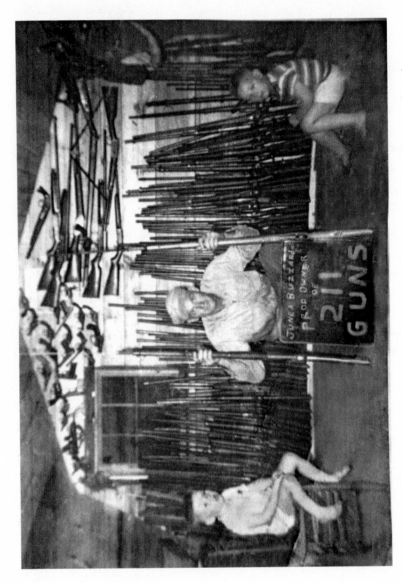

June Buzzard with two of his 14 children proudly displaying his gun collection in the attic of his cabin. (Photograph courtesy of Mrs. Lottie Pyles).

I don't recall what I said next, but that moment is frozen permanently in my memory. Standing in that dark, dusty loft, in a cabin at the end of nowhere with this wonderful, daffy, naïve, crafty man who had just let me into his inner self pushed the boundary of what I knew about human nature way past anything I had ever imagined before. It was no different or less important than seeing, reading or experiencing something that so jolts your attention that it becomes part of how you define the world around you. It's an unexpected opportunity we are sometimes lucky enough to have to break one of our own mental clinches, and truly understand and accept another way of thinking. The accompanying sensation, the affect we feel in that moment, confirms its truth.

When we were back in the clearing I knew I could ask June if I could buy some whiskey from him. We were in a different place than we were before we went up to the loft. I simply asked. There was no longer any anxiety attached to the issue.

"Well, Philip," he said with a chuckle, "I don't make that stuff. My daddy did, and folks 'round here know it, too. But I don't. No, sir, I don't. When folks ask me how come, I say look up yonder." He pointed to the top of a very tall pine tree on the edge of the clearing. It took me a few moments to spot it, but in the uppermost branches I could see a "worm"–the familiar corkscrew copper tubing that topped a still, condensing the vapors to separate water from alcohol.

"That there was my daddy's worm. I put it up there so everyone could see I don't make whiskey. I can't make whiskey without a worm."

I was now part of June's kabuki. "Yes, sir," I said, looking up at the worm, "I can see you don't make it any more. And a damn good thing, too. Still, it would be nice if a man could get some good whiskey. There's so much crap out there, you know? People making pisswater instead of real whiskey. A man would pay top dollar for something decent. That is, if he could get it." I took out some bills and peeled back a five, paused, then a second five. June reached out and tapped the second five with his index finger, then pulled his hand away.

"You know," he said, "You ought to take another trail out of here, Philip. You ought to go up yonder past my cabin toward that ridge. Big ol' oak up there on top. Big one. You could go right around that oak, and follow the ridge on out."

We shook hands, June went back inside with his new Marlin rifle, and I started up the steep trail behind the house. A few hundred yards up there was a large oak, and behind it, under some leaves, a quart Mason jar filled with what looked like water. I left the two fives where the jar had been, and retreated back through the woods to my car.

Sadly, my relationship with June was a short one and I only saw him a few more times over the next two years. We traded a few things, but I didn't buy any more whiskey. Later, while I was still in college, the moonshine question came up again and I said I'd try to get some. But I had a feeling things might not work out. I was not really doing this for myself, and it felt like I would be exploiting a special—if tenuous—relationship. Bad karma. It's one of those memories we all have of paying the price for not listening to a sensible inner voice.

It was around Thanksgiving, and a light snow had fallen. The sky was dark, the wind was picking up, and it felt like a real storm was on the way. The road up to June's was slippery, and the dogs seemed to hear me from the moment I got out of the car. The woodpiles and machinery in the clearing in front of the cabin were covered with snow. The dogs were agitated and instead of standing against the fence as they usually did, they were charging at the wire and slamming into it. I was terrified they would break through the rusted enclosure and come after me. There was no one in sight to call them off.

The only sign of human life was smoke pouring from the chimney. But in spite of the din created by the dogs, no one came out. They have to know I'm here, I thought. Why isn't June coming out?

I thought about running back down the trail, but images of a half a dozen coon dogs running me down stopped me. The only alternative was to knock on the door. But as I approached, I saw the snow in front of the door was laced with blood, bright-red fresh stuff, and lots of it. There seemed to be a trail of blood going around the side of the cabin, either going out or coming in. I couldn't tell which.

Summoning all my courage, I knocked on the door. Nothing. The dogs were making too much noise to tell if there was anything going on in the cabin. I knocked again, a little more forcefully. Nothing. Now what? Make a break for it? Pound on the door?

The door ripped open. June was standing in the doorway holding a bloody hunting knife, a look of anger on his face. He was wearing nothing but a pair of blood-drenched trousers, and his hands and arms were covered with blood. June's wife was standing by the stove lowering something into an enormous pot of boiling water. The children were gathered around a table littered with empty cans, a can lid-roller clamped to one end of the table.

A dead bear lay face up on the floor. Its hide had been pulled back, the carcass partially stripped of meat.

I was stunned by the sight, and sputtered, "My god, June, what are you doing?!"

"I'm canning bear, you damn fool."

He slammed the door in my face. I stumbled and slid as fast as I could back to the car. I never saw June again.

When I started working on this project I was determined to tell the story of my brief interaction with him. But it posed a problem. Obviously, when you tell a story about a man whose life was as dramatic and eccentric as June's was, especially if you also throw in something about bootlegging, you run the risk of upsetting his family, and that is the last thing I wanted to do. At first I didn't have much luck finding or talking with his kin, but I finally got lucky when I met his daughter, Lottie Pyles. Not only was she happy to talk about her dad and show me some of the treasures he left her, she also understood that my intention was to honor a unique man, not in any way diminish his memory. Lottie gave me a wealth of detail about June, and several wonderful stories.

I met June toward the end of his man-in-the-hollow stage. After he sold his cabin he moved into a more open farming area, and became a full-time collector of antiques, particularly glass, bells, cider mills, pottery and bottles. He literally filled an old house with antiques and an entire school bus with bottles. He went after anything that was old. Farm machinery, logging and mining equipment, it didn't matter how big or heavy it was, he collected it.

And of course he continued to collect guns. By the way, his worry about being robbed turned out to be prophetic: one year before he left the cabin, he was robbed. He was away at the time, so no head injury, but the loss was devastating to him.

But he quickly made up for his losses, and the guns he had at the end of his life were high quality firearms, some extremely valuable and unique.

Lottie has his favorite, a Civil War sniper rifle weighing 26 pounds.[18] When people admired the gun, June would say, "You like it? Well, you can have it." Pause for effect. "That is, if you can shoulder that gun and hold 'er up for one minute." Many took the challenge, but no one ever took the gun away from June. The record, by the way, was 40 seconds.

As far as moonshine was concerned, June was definitely out of the business. He did make a little peach wine from time to time, and spiked it with a little white lightening. But June never touched a drop himself.

June was also a master butcher and collected (what else?) old butchering equipment. He began shearing sheep when he was eleven and along with collecting, he raised hogs and owned a meat house. He was also a Navy veteran of WWII, and found time somewhere in the middle of his life to work in the West Virginia coal mines.

You can easily see why I found this man so arresting. You only had to spend a few minutes with him, hear one of his stories, or do a single trade to know you were in the presence of an utterly unique individual. Even in death he had a surprise. He always had coal-black hair. Suddenly, it turned white, and a day later he died.

Chapter XI

Two Gorillas and a Bunch of Snakes

"I'm the last one," Virginia Hiner said. "They're all passed on but me."

She was referring to "my staff", as the Madam called the group of butlers, maids, gardeners and chauffeurs who served so long and faithfully. By the time Grandmother was in her mid-nineties she lived alone at Folly Farm supported by a cook, two maids, a driver, and surrounded by a pack of nasty, heel-biting Welsh Corgies.

And now, thirty-five years after the Madam has gone on to rearrange the Afterworld to her specifications, Virginia was the only direct connection left. I had reconnected with her after a long hiatus with two purposes in mind. First, I wanted to learn more about the invisible realm behind the kitchen doors, specifically Virginia's take on the way they all managed to stay so calm in spite of Grandmother's constantly angry dissatisfaction.

At the same time, I wanted to let Virginia know how grateful I remain for all the times she covered for me when I was about to get in hot water with the Madam. More importantly, though, I intended to thank her for a particular moment when she briefly dropped the servant posture, took a chance, and told a know-it-all ten-year-old something he badly needed to learn. It was reminiscent of Frank Williams' confrontation with the Madam over voting. The difference is, Virginia's response jolted me into seeing something I certainly wasn't going to get from my parents.

It was the fall of 1948 and the presidential election between Dewey and Truman loomed huge in our house. My fiercely Republican family simply hated Harry Truman, and were pinning their hopes on Dewey not only to win, but to reverse the FDR and Harry Hopkins pro-labor, "socialist" programs that were destroying America. Naturally, I heard all of this and assumed everyone was equally excited about dumping Mr. Truman.

One morning I met Virginia in the pantry and asked her if she was going to vote.

"Yes, sir, Mr. Philip, I sure am."

"For Mr. Dewey, right, Virginia?"

"No, Master Philip, for Mr. Truman."

I was horrified! Mr. Truman! How could it be?

"Mr. Philip, there's something you don't understand. In this world there are two kinds of people: rich people and poor people. And there are two kinds of politics: Republican and Democrat. Rich people are Republicans, and poor people are Democrats. Mr. Truman is a Democrat and I'm voting for him."

What a stunning revelation! Up to that moment I had never given a moment's thought to the economic circumstances of the people who worked for us. To be confronted with the idea that they were poor and had no real choice in the matter changed everything. I had always assumed they worked for us because they wanted to. Suddenly, I realized it wasn't so.

No, Virginia didn't remember that moment, but she was glad she said it, and pleased it had an effect on me.

On the issue of coping with the Madam she had a simple answer, one in harmony with what Alice, Martha and others all said. It was a job at a time and in a place where jobs were scarce. And as far as dealing with Grandmother went: "We all stuck together."

Because they worked in day and evening shifts, Virginia was in the habit of talking to whoever just got off to get an idea of what kind of mood the Madam was in that day. One day she called Alice, and by a freak of the party line system, the Madam just happened to be listening in as Alice reported that the Madam was in a particularly foul humor that day. Suddenly, the Madam broke in.

"I heard that, you two!"

Virginia froze, convinced they would both be fired on the spot. But before the Madam could say another word, Alice spoke.

"You know it's true, Mrs. Hirsh. Everything we said is true. You treat us like we are nothing. Someone needs to tell you that."

The Madam hung up. Virginia went to work fully expecting to be fired. But the Madam didn't say a thing. It was never mentioned, and both Alice and Virginia continued to work for Grandmother until she died. And, yes, it did seem like she was less hostile after that, Virginia said.

There were other memories.

"Do you remember the time you took Mrs. Hirsh's steak and blamed it on the dog?" Actually I do remember it, I was thirteen when it happened, and shocked to hear that Virginia knew anything about it. Like candy runs at Calumet, I always thought it was a perfect crime. It was done on impulse without any outside help, leaving behind clues leading straight to a culprit who would be powerless to protest his innocence. It was my little secret, no one knew.

Turns out I was wrong. The only one it fooled was the Madam.

Glenn Williams and I were going camping. Glenn was a little late getting all his chores done, and that meant we had less time before dark to catch a fat fish or shoot a squirrel for dinner at our "hunt club." I had gotten a few things together, put them in the jeep, and was about to go pick up Glenn when it occurred to me there might be some extra food lying around the kitchen. My grandmother was planning a big party that Saturday night, and that always meant plenty of food. Maybe there's something they won't miss.

There in the middle of the kitchen worktable, sitting on a large sheet of gleaming white butcher's paper, stood an enormous chateaubriand. It probably weighed six pounds, enough tenderloin for a dozen guests. Perfect for two hungry campers.

I took the steak and put the butcher's paper on the floor, bloody side up. Then I opened the back door, unhooked one end of the spring on the back porch screen door, and called in Dusty, Grandmother's favorite Great Dane. He immediately went to work on the paper. I jumped in the jeep, threw the steak on the back seat, and took off.

We started to cook the meat as soon as we had a bed of coals in our fireplace. We cooked, waited, and cooked some more. It just didn't want to get done. We sliced pieces off the outside, eating it a bit at a time. By the time we finally went to sleep we had eaten no more than ten percent of the steak. We left it on the dying grill, and resumed eating in the morning. We had to throw most of it away before we went home.

When I got back the Madam was still fuming about the steak. The loss hadn't slowed the party at all; there was always an enormous supply of meat in the freezer house, so the dinner had gone off as expected. What had the Madam so hot was how the doors could have been left open, and how Dusty could still want his dinner after downing that enormous piece of meat. Poor Dusty was not fed that night, so to make it up to him I thawed a brick of horse meat and gave him the entire thing.

It may have buffaloed the Madam, but Virginia and the others weren't fooled for a second. And all these years I thought I had been so clever.

"That's not all you did," Virginia said. "Do you remember how you were always doing something with snakes? Do you remember what you did to me in the kitchen?"

No, I didn't recall, and it worried me I was about to hear that I could have played any sort of mischief on my guardians. It didn't fit the mental image I had constructed around my behavior. They were safe from any mischief; it was the Madam who had to look out. My only defense on this one is age: I was too young to know any better. Virginia didn't buy it.

Walking though the kitchen one afternoon, Virginia spotted one of my socks next to the sink, a knot tied in one end. That's strange, she thought. What is Master Philip's sock doing there? She picked it up, and the sock started to wriggle. She screamed, threw the sock in the air, and when she recovered, went looking for me. She says she made me apologize and free the snake—far from the house. I don't remember it.

That wasn't my first snake-related incident. When I was six I had a mishap involving my mother, one that so upset her she would never—literally all her life—accept that it was an innocent mistake, just extremely bad timing, and I wasn't gunning for her. She never bought it.

I was home alone (meaning without parents; of course, there were servants) one fine spring day playing among the rocks in the woods behind the house. Standing on a boulder with heaven knows what grandiose fantasy in my play-mind, I spotted a small snake on the ground. Investigating, I found a garter snake hatch under the big rock. There were small garter snakes everywhere, and they looked like they were ready to disperse. No time to lose!

I rushed back to the house searching frantically for something to put all the snakes in to hold them until I could get some sort of legitimate cage together. Trouble was, I couldn't find the right container. It had to have a top or these guys would easily slither out. In the basement there was a three-tiered large wooden rack to hold suitcases; there were perhaps fifteen to twenty all neatly lined up and arranged by size. A suitcase! The perfect temporary holding device until I could find something better. So I grabbed one and headed back into the woods.

It was quite a job getting the snakes to stay in the case, but I finally got most of them collected and went back to the house to search for a better box. About that time Mother rolled in the driveway. She hated snakes, so I thought it best to put the suitcase back in its place in the rack, look for a better box, and make the switch when she was out of the way.

What I didn't know was that Dad was going out of town on an unplanned business trip, and she was there to pack a bag for him. A few minutes later I heard Mother screaming from her bedroom. Alice and I arrived at about the same moment, but when she saw a snake, Alice took off leaving me there to hold the bag, so to speak.

Mother was beyond livid. She demanded I catch all the snakes and release them far from the house. The suitcase was thrown away. She was absolutely convinced I had engineered the whole thing as a sick joke, and I was going to be punished severely when Father came home to get his bag. I tried in vain to prove my innocence: be logical, Mother, how in the world could I know you were coming home to pack a bag? And how could I possibly know which bag to put the snakes in?

But she wasn't buying any of it.

When Father got home, he was in a hurry, and in no mood to do anything more than yell at me. Worse—from Mother's point of view—he didn't see how I could have deliberately targeted her with one particular suitcase. She vented about what it was like to open a bag and have twenty snakes fan out across the bedroom. They got in a huge row about it, he stormed out, and Mother spent the night in the guest room. She never let go of the idea I wanted to give her a heart attack.

I have always had the suspicion the snakes-in-the-bag incident played heavily in the decision to send me to Camp Calumet the next summer.

Mother wasn't the only one in our household who hated snakes. Grandfather was convinced that the water snakes in the Jackson River were deadly vipers, cottonmouths who had migrated up the James River from the Great Dismal Swamp. He wanted them dead, and was willing to pay a bounty of 25 cents each. Trouble was, I didn't like killing them; I preferred catching to killing. And besides, I had practically memorized the big snake book in our library, and it said there were no cottonmouths north of the Great Dismal Swamp, and certainly none in the mountains of Bath County. What we had were common brown water snakes. Nasty, nippy and ill-humored, but totally harmless to humans.

He didn't care what the book said, there was a price on their ugly little heads, and if I didn't want to do it, he'd get someone else. It was tempting, but I had to pass on the chance to cash in on his prejudice.

Virginia wondered if I remembered the time just after Glenn Williams arrived when we were thrown out of the County Fair and brought home by the fair's director, Lester Dalton? Snakes again.

The fair that year was held in the old empty Tidewater Hardwood commissary building in Bacova, the one Uncle Malcolm would later convert to a factory for his fiberglass fabricating business, and the place where my grandparents joined hands in the paint spraying machine. The adjacent open fields were perfect for rides and outdoor exhibits, and the huge open interior was equally suited for the cages of rabbits, chickens, ducks and the odd chinchilla, plus rows and rows of giant squash, tomatoes, rutabaga and radishes.

The 4-H kids sold trivets made of popsicle sticks, woven pot holders and hand-sewn aprons, and the ladies from every church around exhibited and sold fruit pies.

It seemed everyone had something hand-made or home-grown to show off. I had neither, but it struck me as a great idea to round up some local snakes and display them. It would be educational, and after all, wasn't that a theme of the event? While it made sense to me, it didn't to the fair director and County Agent, Mr. Dalton. It was like talking to Mother. Or a brick wall.

I complained to Father about the lockout, and suddenly Mr. Dalton allowed as how it would be all right if Glenn and I had a small display. But there were restrictions: the snakes had to be in a proper cage from which escape was impossible, they had to be displayed on the second floor away from the rabbits and guinea hens, and if anyone complained they had to go. Understood?

The fair lasted a week, it was already the third day, and Mr. Dalton knew we didn't have a proper cage—to say nothing of the fact we had yet to catch the first reptile. I think he figured it was a safe bet we would never make it to the second floor of the commissary. He didn't realize that when it came to cages and snakes, he was up against pros.

We made the box out of wide oak planks. The front was a single piece of salvaged glass, the sides were riddled with wire-covered holes to allow air to circulate, and the entire back was the door, hinged at the top. It looked great, but at that point we should have spotted the design flaw and moved the hinges. It would have saved a lot of trouble.

The snake part was relatively easy. We wanted a variety to make it especially educational so we scoured the woods and riverbank, and caught a hognose, a couple of garters, a small rat snake, and several brown water snakes. Granted, we were a bit over-balanced with water snakes, but they were plentiful, we were in a hurry, and we didn't think anyone would really care.

In the afternoon of the fifth day of the fair Frank Williams delivered us and our display. I could already picture the blue ribbon on top of the box. We were a cinch to win; after all, there was no competition.

Because all the good space had been taken up with rhubarb and giant sun flowers, we were told the only place we could put the box was on a small table against the railing surrounding the stairwell. It was the only way in or out of the second floor, and because the back of the box was over the deepest part of the stair well, people coming up couldn't see it until after they were on the second floor. Even then, they had to move around the stairwell into the large open room to see what was in the box.

I was surprised that so few people seemed interested in the snakes. While no one really objected, few ventured close enough to peer inside. The next day was a Friday, and by mid-afternoon the place was packed. Judges were inspecting the cucumbers, kids were slurping snow cones, and the band was setting up on the lawn.

But there was trouble in the snake box. First of all, the water snakes had all rolled in a ball in the fake pond, displacing all the water into the surrounding dirt producing a large mud hole. Moisture inside the humid box had condensed on the glass front making it impossible to see anything inside. We decided the best course of action would be to open the back, reach in, and wipe off at least the upper half of the glass. The snakes seemed torpid like snakes always do when you look at them at the zoo.

It might have worked if the hinges were on the bottom instead of the top, and it would have helped if the back of the box had been more accessible. But it was standing against the railing over the stairwell, and to clean the glass I had to lean out over the open space, open the door with one hand, and reach inside with the other without either agitating the snakes or falling over the railing. Everything was going just fine until I tried to reach in with the rag to wipe the glass. It was simply too much of a reach, I slipped, jolting the cage. That instantly brought every snake to life, and they all headed for the open door at the same moment. In a lot less time than it takes to tell it, six snakes shot out into the open stairwell, down onto the heads of the people going up and down the stairs.

"SNAKES!!" someone screamed. Then it was bedlam. The snakes were slithering all over the stairs. People upstairs couldn't go down, and they were yelling and acting like they were trapped in a fire. The lower floor cleared out in a heartbeat. Glenn and I ran down the stairs trying to grab the snakes before they could get behind any displays on the first floor.

Suddenly Mr. Dalton appeared. Arms folded, his face red with anger, he watched us frantically grabbing snakes. He didn't say a word until we had all the snakes back in the box.

"Bring that goddamn thing down here and put it in my truck." He drove us home in deadly silence. My parents were standing on the porch when we pulled up.

"I don't want it here," Mother said, pointing toward the barn. But the meter had run out on the Dalton taxi. He wasn't going another inch with us and the Medusa box. He left. Glenn and I lugged the box up to the barn, and released the snakes.

So if you've ever wondered why there are never any snakes displayed at the Bath County Fair, you now know.

In fact, there are a number of things you won't find at the local fairs any more. I especially miss the Gorilla Challenge and the Hoochie-Coochie show, the former a casualty of liability and animal rights concerns, the latter done in by the passing of respect for the good old-fashioned bribe. My grandfather called it "giving the cumshaw," a generous tip to grease the way.

There were really three kinds of country fair, each with a specific purpose and its own set of rules. The fair in Bacova was a clean, 4H family event. Nothing radical: a lot of socializing around the sheep pen, perhaps a local country band, and four or five plywood booths testing your skill at popping balloons with a dart, tossing a rope ring over a stick, or snagging the prize-winning duck with a child's fishing rod. Everyone with an over-sized turnip could win a ribbon in the agriculture exhibit.

Then there was the state fair. No one in Bath went to Richmond for the Virginia State Fair; instead, we went to the West Virginia State Fair just over the line in near-by Fairlea. That was a huge event with massive displays of farm machinery, livestock exhibits (no snakes), and a colorful midway with major attractions like the Terrifying Transformation (beautiful girl turns into a gorilla, rips open its cage and heads for the audience. Everyone screams and bolts for the exit), and the guys who rode motorcycles inside a huge barrel.

The third type was the traveling carnival, usually with a name ending in "Bros." Colorful flyers made it look like Ringling Bros., Clyde Beatty, or the Cole Bros. Circus was on the way. The reality was quite different. Battered trucks driven by filthy "carnies" rolled into town towing all manner of trailers loaded down with rides, food stands and dented Air Streams.

They set up on the baseball field above Hot Springs where the Homestead's all-black baseball team and the town's all-white team played. Both, by the way, were great teams, successfully playing other town and industry teams for literally 100 miles around. But they never played each other.

Everyone turned out to watch the set-up. It really was quite amazing to see a bunch of skinny, sullen, unshaven men bolt together the Teacup Ride, a Ferris wheel, the Rocket Ride (the one that killed Uncle Jack), and the Monster Swing. I was never too keen on the rides; even the Ferris wheel made me nauseous. But it was fun to wander through the crowd eating cotton candy—a rare treat—and watching people stagger cross-eyed off the Monster Swing.

I remember one particularly bizarre moment at the Monster Swing. Next to the Ferris wheel, it was the biggest ride in the fair.

The all-black Homestead Giants baseball team. (Photograph courtesy of Mr. Roger Anderson).

A large central tower perhaps twenty feet tall supported four long arms from which play swings were suspended, five or six per arm. A red snow fence enclosed the entire operation to keep people from getting kicked in the face as the swing heated up. When everyone was seated, the apparatus started to turn, slowly gaining speed until reaching maximum velocity. As the speed increased, riders were lifted up and out until the swings were nearly horizontal. Standing at the snow fence, one could look up and see feet whirling directly overhead.

A large crowd stood watching. I was pressed against the fence watching my friends circling, glad to be on the ground. Suddenly, one of the riders lost his dinner, sending a bilious gush of vomit outward in an enormous spiral over the heads of people standing by the fence but onto the unfortunates at the back of the crowd. In no more than a few seconds, and perhaps one full circle, dozens were splattered.

It confirmed everything I ever thought about paying good money to ride in a circle, horizontal, vertical or any combination of the two.

Then there was the Hoochie Coochie show. As soon as the set up was under way, the older men would start asking the carnies if there was going to be a show that night? Some of the carnies played dumb, some said maybe, but part of the hype was to keep the whole thing no more than a possibility. As the evening wore on, rumors would spread: the cops were watching—no show. Or: wait until the sheriff goes to his car—that's the signal.

Then suddenly the word would spread: the tent behind the concession stand, or perhaps in the little commissary tent. Wherever it was, it was out of the lights, and as far from the crowd as possible. There was no barker at the door, and no tickets sold, just a man collecting dollar bills. Age was no consideration. As long as you had a buck, you were in.

As soon as the tent was packed, the flap was closed, and the "show" began. Usually there was an elevated stage made of a couple of sheets of plywood on some cinder blocks against one wall of the tent. Two or three lights along the front edge pointed roughly toward the back of the platform, just enough to define an audience and a performance area. That kept the crowd at bay, and gave the artist enough room to move without coming within touching distance of the audience. The only other thing on stage was a small 45 RPM record player, the kind with a tiny turntable and a thick center post on which records could be stacked; this one only held one record.

A middle-aged woman wearing a shirt, shorts and sandals stepped through a tent flap at the back of the stage, leaned over and turned on the record player. As Jo Stafford started to sing Shrimp Boats Are A-Coming, the woman began to strip. She didn't smile or seem to make any eye contact with the audience, nor did she make the slightest attempt to dance. Her knees bent slightly in a sort of desultory rhythm, and every fifteen or twenty seconds she turned a bit to the left or the right.

But that was it. She just stripped.

She slid out of her sandals and nudged them together at the back of the little stage with her foot. Next, came the shirt. She unbuttoned it, pulled it off, and tossed it on top of her sandals, all at the same speed and with the same enthusiasm as someone getting ready for bed. She struggled a bit with the bra clasp—that made the audience anxious—the song was moving along (Won't you hurry, hurry, hurry home. . .) and time was getting short.

Finally, there they were: breasts! Two of them! And she was going for the pants! No belt, button or clasp to slow this part. She simply pulled down her shorts and panties in one motion, then tossed them on top of the other clothes. While the song played on (. . .there's dancin' tonight) she continued the suggestion of movement, her eyes focused well over our heads as she turned slowly from side to side to give everyone a look.

Less than a minute later the song was over. The man standing next to me jabbed me in the side with his elbow.

"Here's the good part," he said excitedly.

The woman stepped calmly to the back of the stage, and bent over to gather her clothes and reset the record for the next performance. The "good part" only lasted a few seconds before she ducked through the tent flap. The entire show—start to finish—lasted less than three minutes, but judging from the murmurs of approval, it was a big success. We filed out quickly, another group already formed for the next act.

When I went back to the fair the next afternoon, the dancer was taking tickets for the Kiddie Train, the same look of boredom on her face.

The other now-passed sensation was the Gorilla (pronounced GO-rilla) Challenge. I only saw it once, but I will never forget the experience. The basic hype was big money—fifty bucks—for anyone who could stay in the cage with the Go-rilla for three minutes. That night there were two cages and two Go-rillas, take your pick. Both Go-rillas were in reality chimps, one considerably larger than the other. The smaller cage measured perhaps six feet wide, seven feet tall, and ten feet long. The door was at one end, and the smaller chimp sat folded up on a shelf at the far end, boxing gloves on his feet. He seemed oblivious to the crowd surrounding the cage to watch the challenge.

The bigger chimp's cage was slightly taller, lacked a sitting shelf, and in the middle had a metal bar suspended from the top on chains; quite literally, a monkey bar. This chimp sat in the far corner, gloves on his feet, seemingly asleep.

The barker worked the crowd looking for someone to take the challenge and make some easy money. George Bryant's older brother, Whimpy, seemed a natural. He was tough, strong, and with plenty of encouragement from his friends, he was ready to take on the Go-rilla. He chose the smaller one.

He put on the gloves and stepped bravely into the cage. At the whistle, the big three-minute clock started. Whimpy crouched into a defensive posture, gloves milling slowly in front of his face and upper chest. But the chimp didn't seem to notice.

"You got him, Whimpy," everyone shouted, and, indeed it did look like Whimpy was going to walk off unscratched with the prize money. He wisely stayed near the door, crouched and waiting, but the monkey stayed on his shelf. The seconds ticked by, and as the big hand swept nearer to the three-minute mark, the crowd cheered louder. The barker kept exhorting the monkey to move, but he continued to languish on the shelf.

Then suddenly, with fifteen seconds to go, the chimp shot off the shelf, and in one long leap hit Whimpy square in the chest, knocking him backwards into the cage door. The monkey bounded back to his perch, and Whimpy—thoroughly dazed—was dragged out and given some water.

Recalling the incident recently, Whimpy told me he thinks the barker had a way to give the chimp an electric shock. Whatever the method, Whimpy didn't see it coming, and he says it took a couple of hours to shake it off.

The next volunteer wasn't as lucky.

Seeing what the little chimp did to Whimpy, no one wanted to take on the bigger one. The barker offered to double the money to $100. Some of the boys who had had a few convinced Marvin (not his real name) to take on the Go-rilla; after all, $100 was a whole lot of money. Marvin was bigger and probably quite a bit stronger than Whimpy, and in spite of the alcohol discount, he seemed to have a reasonable chance of lasting three minutes.

"Stay away from him!" people yelled as Marvin stepped into the cage. The chimp opened his eyes, looked Marvin over, and seemed to go back to sleep. Marvin stayed close to the door end of the cage, but unlike Whimpy, he moved back and forth, sparring at the air, bobbing and ducking to keep the animal from having an easy target. It's best to have a strategy when you're facing a Go-rilla.

As before, the monkey seemed oblivious to Marvin. At the two-minute mark he stood up and stretched, but made no move in Marvin's direction. Thirty seconds to go and Marvin was on the move, back and forth, ready for anything. Fifteen seconds. Ten seconds.

"You got him, Marvin!! You got him!!" It looked like the monkey wasn't in the mood to take on the crafty challenger.

Then as suddenly as the first chimp dove off his shelf, the mighty Go-rilla leaped up to the monkey bar, grabbed it with both hands, and swung toward Marvin. His gloved feet shot out together catching Marvin exactly under the chin, knocking him out cold. The monkey retreated to his corner, and Marvin's friends dragged him out of the cage.

The barker's money was safe again.

Chapter XII

Lessons Learned

Sometimes we run into a story I call a "lesson-moment," a tale that no matter how entertaining or rich in metaphor is at its heart a concrete and very useful lesson. We remember almost all of our stories episodically, some get lost for years at a time until something triggers a memory. But a select few stay with us most of the time, especially the straightforward ones that remind us of a moment either when something obscure became clear, or we stumbled onto a fundamental rule of conduct that really works. The principle of *res ipsor loquitor* applies: the thing speaks for itself. No fancy mental gyrations needed, no withdrawals from the memory bank required. This is what it says it is. The story reinforces it, but the lesson stands alone.

I count three particular tales among my best little lesson-moments: one from the hollow, one from the garage, and one seen through the cracks in the wall of a weathered old house.

When I was somewhere around 11 or 12, like every kid that age, I began to try to figure out what this forbidden but enticing thing called sex was all about. My classmates and friends weren't yet talking directly about it. Not much useful information there.

Playboy hadn't hit the news stand, and no one in my family ever made reference to sex.

Growing up on the farm allowed plenty of opportunity to see animals mating and calves and sheep born, but it was hard to make the leap from barnyard to bedroom. It all looked a little gross to me, and no one on the farm offered any explanations. They all seemed rather ho-hum about it. No help there.

The dirty joke was actually the main instrument of early sexual learning. On the farm I sometimes heard a joke or veiled reference to someone who might have had congress with a sheep. With a sheep! Dear God, who would do such a thing? And if he did, how in the world could it be done? It made no sense, and the image was too repulsive for words.

In school, the jokes were closer to the mark, enticing fragments suggesting this was the most thrilling thing one could imagine—if only one knew enough to build a workable fantasy. Like all of my friends, the last place I would go for instruction was my father. No way! Far better to extrapolate from jokes, keep one's ear to the ground and put it together a little bit at a time.

But Father somehow decided it was time to intervene. Maybe it was just an age thing: I was old enough to be told. Maybe he somehow sensed my curiosity. More likely, my mother put him up to it. Whatever the reason, one Saturday morning when I was doing my best to avoid him, he hunted me down and announced we were going for a drive. He said he had to go to some store an hour away and wanted company. I instantly knew better.

Whenever there was something grim afoot, if he didn't blast me outright, we went to the mobile classroom—the car. It suited him to trap me in the front seat and, with eyes straight ahead, tell me something about my behavior that needed to be changed. The only clue I had about how much trouble I was in was the anticipated length of the journey. A two-hour round trip was deadly serious.

These rides always started out with small talk, the warm-up phase to get me ready. Then suddenly, the pounce!

"I think it's time we had a little talk about . . . sex." First a pause, then the question: "What do you know about it?"

"Not much," I mumbled.

"All right, I'll tell you what you need to know." And that was the start of a lecture that droned on all the way to Fisher's Tackle Shop and back. At first it was about men and women being attracted to each other, but the reasons seemed related to the need to marry and have a family. It was as if there existed a timetable for these things: it was time to select a mate, someone from the right jurisdiction with the proper credentials. So far, nothing here about how we get to the part I saw in the barnyard.

But finally we got to it, the "it" being intercourse. Here's where the train left the tracks. By nature and inclination, Father was an engineer. He always carried a slide rule and seemed able to solve any problem with the magic of numbers. And so it was with sex. It had to do with the concept of "entry," the function of "angles," and the scary idea of "penetration." Just where and with what all this entry stuff was happening remained a mystery. Even more obscure was why any two people would want to undertake such a complex and seemingly perilous behavior. Is having children worth all of this?

The longer the descriptions went on the more cross Father seemed to become. By the time his speech ended, I was convinced we were all being conned. The jokes were just that—jokes. It wasn't real, sex was an illusion, a way to make something unpleasant seem desirable. Sheep and dogs liked it, but for people it was far too involved to be any fun.

But it was almost over. We were only minutes away from the driveway. I was glad to be able to say I'd never do it. I promise. Just let me out of here.

But it wasn't to be. "Okay, now tell me: do you have any questions?" Knowing Father as I did, I knew this was not really a question. It was a demand. If I had said, "No, sir, none at all. Thank you for telling me all of this, it really helps," he would have taken my head off. No, there had to be one (and just one) question, a sure sign that I had listened. He'd give me an answer, we could turn in the driveway, and I could disappear. First, I had to come up with one really good question.

That's where I made my big mistake. I actually asked what was on my mind. Noting just how complex the angle of entry issue was, I asked—in total sincerity—the obvious question. "When you want to do "intercourse," do you have to go to a doctor to be put together?"

He exploded. "Jesus Christ! Of course not!" We turned into the driveway and came to a stop. I reached for the handle.

"One more thing," he said in angry-storm voice. "Masturbation! It means 'self-abuse.' It's a dirty word for a dirty thing and I never want you to do it!"

Thus endeth the lesson.

That's where it stayed for several weeks until we went back to the farm for a short visit. One afternoon I was in the garage with my grandmother's chauffeur, Mann, helping him change the oil in one of the cars. He brought up the subject of dating and asked me why I wasn't out with the girls? It didn't feel the least bit awkward to be asked and I told him that, like all my friends, we saw each other in dancing school and birthday parties and, sure, I liked Joan a lot, but just how to approach this dating thing seemed overwhelming. After all, I couldn't drive and about the only way to "date" was to be driven to a movie and back home. Big deal.

Mann then started to fill in the gaps by actually talking about what we called "petting." The way he talked about it, it was something that both boys and girls liked—a startling piece of information—but the big trick was just how you negotiate what and how far it will go. "You gotta start slow," he advised, "and some day down the road you'll just know when it's time to go all the way, and make love."

Love? Me? What about the angles, the children, all of that?

Over the next hour or so in a straightforward manner Mann filled me in. And it all made perfect sense. Even so, at the end I had to ask him a question, a real question.

"Tell me: just how much fun is making love?"

We were both sitting on the workbench. Mann turned, put his hand on my shoulder, and with a huge grin said the magic words, "Believe me, you're gunna love it!" His grin was so real, so deeply felt, that I finally got it.

Of course, he was right.

And so was Leo Lockridge, but the lesson was different. When Leo was the sheriff of Bath County he was also its leading auctioneer. I remember him as an older man who used a cane. I never saw him wearing a sheriff's uniform, and I couldn't imagine Leo chasing down any bad guys. Bath was a quiet place, and there weren't any moonshiners left.

One Saturday afternoon a big auction was held way up a hollow on a small farm. The owner had died and all of his possessions were lined up in rows in the front yard. Every frying pan, table and farm implement from tractors to boxes of rusty nails were to be auctioned off, and Leo was there to make it go fast and fetch the best possible price. I was trading with June Buzzard at the time, and one of the items I dearly wanted was an old Winchester .38-40 rifle, just the sort of thing to coax June into some real trading.

During a brief pause I told Leo just how badly I wanted that rifle, and not to let it go without giving me a shot at the best bid. As the crowd moved down the row closer to the gun I was distracted by a brief conversation, and when I turned back I saw someone walking away with my rifle. I was incensed and rudely interrupted Leo.

"Mr. Lockridge! I wanted to bid on that gun!"

"Well, son," he said, "Just goes to show: you gotta keep your eye on the gobbler." And he resumed his auction chant.

Keep my eye on the gobbler! What the hell was that all about? One of the old timers who saw my dismay and confusion straightened me out. It all had to do with a turkey shoot.

I knew a "turkey shoot" as an event at a fair or picnic. You paid a quarter for a small piece of paper about the size of a birthday card with an "X" in the middle. At your turn you nailed it to a post, stood back twenty yards or so, and took one blast at it with a shotgun, scattering tiny pellet holes across the target. The person who got a pellet closest to the exact center of the "X" won a prize of some sort. Just what it had to do with turkeys was a bit unclear, it certainly had nothing to do with skill: it was just luck.

In the old days, the man explained, turkey shoots were a serious matter and involved considerable skill. The prize was a real (dead) turkey. Turkey shoots dated back to colonial times when people used flintlocks and percussion black powder guns. A turkey was tethered behind a big log fifty yards or more from the shooters. Corn was scattered behind the log and when the bird pecked at the corn it was hidden from view. But turkeys are wary creatures, and while they eat they periodically stand up straight, take a quick look around, then duck back to the food. The marksman had to get a bead and shoot in the few seconds the turkey's head was visible above the log. Turns were taken until someone hit the turkey—then the bird was his.

That's where the expression originated: Keep your eye on the gobbler.

Finally, there is the story of Carl and Roy Swearengin, a tale with several points worth taking.

Just because the Great Depression ended with WWII doesn't mean that prosperity instantly spread across the land, especially so in the depths of Appalachia where unemployment was nearly universal, and starvation an ugly, continuing reality. Roy and Carl were 11 and 12 respectively when their parents told them they had to leave Virginia to find work. The boys' father had tried to make it cutting pulpwood for the mill in Covington about fifty miles away, but lacking a good truck and not being able to cut enough wood for the family forced their parents to factory jobs in New Jersey.

Their home was in poor shape, and Carl told me you could look outside through the cracks in any wall in the house. Before leaving, their father got a barrel of flour and hung a half a hog in the smokehouse. An uncle who lived about ten miles away was to look in on the boys every month or so. Otherwise, they were on their own. Even at the age of 12 Carl didn't take it to mean they were being abandoned. He and his brother knew what hard times were, and they would simply have to cope with it.

They knew their food wouldn't last too long, and they had to figure out some way to make money. They hoed corn for 25 cents a day, but that was seasonal and they knew they would have to find something they could do all year. Since their father had been a pulpwood cutter, they knew how to fell a tree, trim it with an ax, and using a two-man saw, cut it into six-foot pieces for the mill. They had a neighbor, Pete Cauley, who had a truck and they struck a deal with him. When they had enough wood for a truckload Pete would haul it to Covington and split the money with the boys.

So they set to work. Using a dog chain, ax and their father's saw, they cut wood and tumbled it down the hill to the road, piling it up along the road until they thought they had enough for a load. Nope, said Mr. Cauley, not enough. Back to work. They cut wood all day, and fed themselves at night. Every meal was the same. First a piece of "side meat" was fried over the fire, and as grease accumulated, flour and water were added making a kind of bread-thick gravy, or "skillet bread" as the boys called it. They supplemented their diet with poke salad, berries and apples. Even in winter they could "kick up apples in the snow," a common Depression-era way to find food.

It took one month of labor, but they finally had a load. They loaded Mr. Cauley's truck and when he returned they were looking at $24.00! "I remember it like it was yesterday. It was more money than we ever saw before. We thought we were millionaires." So they did what they thought rich people would do: they hitchhiked to the city to celebrate. The city, in this case, was Clifton Forge about forty miles away. They had never seen a movie or smelled popcorn before. They saw every movie several times over, ate candy and popcorn until they were sick, then hitchhiked home.

"Trouble was," Carl said, "We forgot to buy groceries. And it took another month to get up a load of wood." The "side meat" and flour gave out about two weeks into the second month. "I'll tell you, we 'bout starved to death in them last two weeks." But they finally got a load, Mr. Cauley hauled it, and they had another $24.00. "This time, we bought groceries first. Then we each put a dollar in our pocket, and spent the rest in Clifton Forge. We never went hungry again." In telling the story Carl arched up in his chair, and patted his right front pocket, and smiled.

"Ever since then, I always keep one dollar in my pocket. Yes, sir, just remember: never spend your last dollar."

Chapter XIII

Skunk in the Lobby

There is no way one can tell stories about the land of many springs without underlining the importance of the Homestead Hotel. When the American Revolution started, the hotel—in its earliest form—was already ten years old. It was established at the same time as the first American medical school, and 59 years before Thomas Jefferson's beloved University of Virginia opened its doors. The hotel is going strong 238 years later, still the dominant force in the life and economy of Bath.

Until recent times it was hard to find anyone whose job or livelihood didn't depend in some way on the hotel. Before the railroad came in the late nineteenth century, specialty goods, spirits and staples were all brought in by difficult over-land routes. Everything else was grown, raised and bought locally. The hotel maintained an enormous dairy herd, farmed thousands of acres of grain fields, and raised beef, poultry, lamb and pork. Except for the decade or so when the Tidewater Hardwood Company was afloat, directly or indirectly the hotel has always busied most of the area's work force.

From its earliest days, there has been no place remote enough in Bath County to get beyond the needs or influence of the hotel. Floyd Cleek's father, Eli (1840–1902), for example, was known to be the county's best butcher, and the only one allowed to touch the hotel's veal. When there was work to be done, a rider and horse were sent for Mr. Cleek. He was paid in cash, unusual in an economy almost entirely based on barter. Until the early twentieth century the hotel was the only major source of cash seeping into the system.

There have been many resort hotels in the area, but the Homestead is the only major survivor. Virtually every large spring in the area has some sort of spa history, some quite elaborate.[19] Curiously, early tourism was not the driving force behind the popularity of the spas; that didn't become a factor until well into the twentieth century. No, there were two far more powerful issues that drove people from as far away as New England to undertake the arduous journey to a frontier spa. First there was health, and the desperate lengths people would go to find it; second, there was something people would go to equally great lengths to avoid: mosquitoes.

The vast coastal wetlands were a major problem for early settlers. Travelers had to go out of their way to circumnavigate soggy river bottoms, sloughs and swamps. The Great Dismal Swamp on the Virginia-North Carolina border, for example, was an impenetrable 900 square mile snake-infested mosquito quagmire. And it was just one of thousands of similar though smaller coastal sloughs and lowland bogs, all cranking out mosquitoes by the billion.

Draining and filling wetlands to create more tillable land took a tremendous amount of time, energy and vital resources. Wetlands were hard to hunt and fish, and made nearby farms vulnerable to flood during periods of heavy rain. Today, we suffer devastation from the occasional fall hurricane; imagine the effect Hugo would have had in 1760.

Wetlands also meant mosquitoes, thick clouds of ravenous insects blanketing the country searching for blood. They traveled in huge cone-shaped swarms, literally billions of hungry diseased bugs whose only instinct was to aspirate enough blood to get the strength to reproduce. Only the tiniest fraction of one percent ever scored a corpuscle. The rest simply died off, fell in a creek and became an *hors d'oeuvre* for a sunfish. No one had a can of OFF in those days. Burning St. Louis sagebrush or white ash was a way to drive them away from your house, and rubbing the juice of the witch shrub (*Hamamelis virginiana*—good old witch hazel) on a bite could provide a little relief. But when the 'skeeters were really bad it meant heavy clothes, gloves, and layers of mud caked on exposed skin.

Along with mosquitoes came disease. No one quite knew the why of it, but there was a prevailing sense that mosquitoes made people sick. In South Carolina, the well-to-do in the capital, Columbia, made for Charleston in the summer because there seemed to be less Yellow Fever and Malaria on the coast. It was thought that the salt air was somehow protective, but the real reason was the sandy soil: it didn't hold water, and there were fewer standing puddles to breed mosquitoes.

The other escape was altitude. An early Homestead ad proclaimed "America's Greatest Health Resort" a "Cure for Rheumatism, Gout and Nervous Diseases," and guaranteed the hotel to be "Free from Mosquitoes."

The spa was not simply a treatment method for one illness or another. It could also prevent disease so one didn't get gleet, dropsy, or biliousness in the first place. And everyone wanted to avoid the medical profession—doctors and barbers in those days— and the draconian ways they treated the sick. Their methods ranged from mild but harmless plant extracts and non-toxic chemicals to the induction of vomiting, cleansing the innards with horrendous salt-laced enemas, or the sure-fire cure of bloodletting. The red and white barber's pole originated as the way barbers advertised their skill: the red stripe for blood, the white for the tourniquet. The unlucky patient's vein was opened with a sharp (and presumably dirty) lancet, and blood was allowed to drip into what looked like a sommelier's tasting cup. The flow was stanched when the patient grew faint.

George Washington was bled to death by otherwise well-meaning physicians who relieved him of most of his blood in less than twenty-four hours. George was almost certainly a goner anyway—he seems to have had an overwhelming strep infection—but draining him did nothing but make embalming easier.

Likewise vomiting and enemas: the last thing you want when ill is to lose vital electrolytes and fluids, to say nothing of the all-too-frequent ruptured bowel caused by the over-zealous application of an enema syringe.

No question about it: bobbing about in a hot spring in the mosquito-free mountains was a lot better way to approach prevention and infirmity. Even the threat of Indian raids didn't discourage the afflicted. The last Indian raid was in 1783, twenty-two years after a bathhouse was built over one of the two Warm Springs, and seventeen years after Thomas Bullitt (formerly an officer at Fort Dinwiddie) opened his "rustic cabins" in the middle of what is now the Homestead Hotel.[20] In 1750—sixteen years before Bullitt—an early explorer wrote in his journal that he encountered "Six Invalides" taking the waters in the Warm Springs.

Enough people ignored the dangers and difficulties of travel to allow Bullitt's hotel and the twelve other area hostelries, inns, and spas to prosper in the latter part of the 18th century. That was in part because they all shared the same customers who visited springs in succession. The custom of the day was to stay at each spring for several days—even weeks—then move on to the next. Not all springs were alike, and guests were well versed in the reputed virtue of each specific spring. Thus, one arranged visits in timed sequence to gain the maximum benefit of each stay.

Comfort mattered, but the therapeutic value of each individual spring was the real drawing card. Still, as early as the end of the 18th century, some of the resorts featured resident drama companies, orchestras, and nightly dances.

The Warm Springs bathhouse still stands, and is possibly the oldest structure of its kind in the country. Somewhere around 1810 a grand hotel named the Colonnade (perhaps punning on its superiority to the dread enema) opened its doors above the pools. Thomas Jefferson was a regular at both "The Warm" (as it was known), and the Homestead. Washington probably took a dip on one or both of his visits to Fort Dinwiddie, though it would have been just before the bathhouse went up.[21]

Bathing was a precise process starting with the costume (fancy hat, slippers and robe), then the timing of one's bath. Though it varied over the years, there was a generally understood limit beyond which the healthy influence of the waters suddenly reversed itself. Fifteen to twenty minutes twice a day was considered perfect. Thirty minutes was the edge of no-man's land beyond which lay the risk of organ failure. Everyone knows that too much good food makes you sick, and excessive use of even the best medicines can be toxic. So don't monkey around with immersion in a hot, sulfurous-smelling pool.

There is another phenomenon of the hot spring that should be mentioned: each spring has its own persona, a personality one can see, smell, feel, and taste. When you walk through the slightly crooked door into the Warm Springs pool, for example, you are immediately in another world. The ancient floorboards of the narrow perimeter walkway boom under your feet as you make your way around to a tiny dressing room. The pool is forty feet across, six feet deep, and crystal clear. The steam that rises through the open roof has a slightly rotten-egg smell, and the water (once said to be healthy to drink) tastes bitter and has a nasty lingering aftertaste.

A slippery narrow stairway takes you down into a tiny grotto where you can sit on a stone step, and yell up to the attendant who will open the gates above and let a thunderous stream of hot water pound your back. You have to hold onto a rope hanging from the wall to keep from being swept off your perch.

There is no crowd, no line, and no wait. Sitting on that ancient rock, alone, with hot water pounding on your back feels to me like stepping over the ropes at a museum to live a few private moments in history. It is an unhurried, utterly unique experience.

The idea of taking the waters to excess was still alive and well when I was a kid. Small cardboard clocks with movable hands were tacked next to each dressing room. Horrace, the attendant, would set the time of everyone's stay and watch to be certain it did not exceed the safe thirty-minute limit. The bath was always followed by rapid immersion in a pool of icy-cold water flowing from a spring next to the larger warm springs. It was supposed to counter the soporific effect of the bath so you would leave feeling refreshed.

But if Horrace turned his back, I would immediately jump back into the hot pool. It was a very daring thing to do, not because it could irritate Horrace into complaining to my parents, but because the sudden change from ice water to hot water made your skin burn for a few moments. Fairly harmless by today's standards, but at the time it was pretty racy.

My family always considered the Homestead to be their personal country club, an attitude shared by other wealthy local gentry. There is a story I often heard as a kid about one particularly eccentric man named Kenneth Ellis. He had no patience with any convention, including the Homestead's black-tie-after-six rule. Supposedly, he walked into the lobby one evening wearing work clothes and mud-covered hobnailed boots. The manager, Mr. Lennon, rushed up to him and said with alarm: "Mr. Ellis! Sir! You can't come in here dressed like that! You'll have to leave at once!"

Mr. Ellis is alleged to have said—without breaking stride or even looking at Mr. Lennon—"Shut up, Lennon, or I'll buy the place and fire you." Did it happen? I don't know, but the tale was often repeated, and true or not became a sort of parable to explain "our" position vis-à-vis the hotel.

Family friends would often come for the entire summer known as the social season so there was always a ready supply of golf and drinking partners. Some rented a cottage on Cottage Row, which came with its own servants and access to every comfort the hotel had to offer; others preferred accommodation in the hotel itself. One of the Madam's friends, a woman with the unlikely name of The Countess Chittadini, sent workers ahead to tear out walls to make a suitable suite for the Countess and her many dogs. At the end of the social season, she had the space restored.

Somewhere in the 1950's the number of summer-long dwellers fell off enough to put the hotel in a financial pinch. Then the unthinkable happened: business conventions were allowed during social season! My parents and grandparents were outraged. How could this be? Our playground besmirched by common business riff-raff!! What's next? Relax the black-tie-after-six rule? At first the hotel promised it was only for August. But it wasn't long before July fell, then June, and the idea of "social season" was history.

But like it or not, it was still the only game in town. Most of the wealthy season-long veterans either bought houses in the county or moved to some other resort. My parents grumbled, but made the adjustment. Even so, they never stopped complaining about the degrading effect on the Hot of registering commoners, often referred to as "NOCD" (Not Our Class, Dear).

Over the years my parents went less and less, especially after they grew too old to play golf. The last time I went with them they put on a profoundly allegorical performance that summed up both their attitude toward the hotel, and their feeling about lesser beings in general.

It began rather nicely: it was the summer of 1993 and our son, Ian, had just been graduated from college. My father invited us all to go to the Homestead to celebrate with a formal dinner in the Grand Dining Room. I dug out my best suit, my wife bought a new black dress, and after cocktails we readied ourselves for the drive to the hotel. So far, so good. Only one little chore left: let the dog—an ancient but still-feisty Jack Russell named Ruff—out to pee.

Six feet out the back door he ran straight into a skunk. The skunk gave him a point-blank rectal blast, some of which rolled through the open door in a nauseating fog.

Unless you live on the north slope of Alaska, you have certainly smelled a dead skunk on the highway. Sometimes the odor is faint. Nasty, to be sure, but brief and quite tolerable. Sometimes it's pungent, lingering, and has a "Dear God! That stinks!" quality. And you think you've smelled the worst this bushy-tailed parfumeur has to offer.

Well, you're wrong. There is a third level of olfactory injury, exponentially worse than anything you have ever wiffed on the highway. To get it, you must be within range of an aimed blast, close enough to get a few drops of the stuff on your face and clothes. At that range it is no longer a "smell" at all. It is a nauseating, tear-making, throat-closing, breath-stopping assault as overpowering as a blast of tear gas and pepper spray combined.

And when it happens to a dog, the first thing it will do is race along with its face on the ground trying to rub the offending agent out of its eyes. And that is exactly what Ruff did, only instead of using the lawn as a rubbing blotter, he shot back into the house and zig-zagged frantically back and forth across Father's favorite Persian rug.

"Let's get out of here," I said to Ian, and we headed out the opposite side of the house to get into some fresh air. Even though we were well away from the door where the skunk fog blew in, and our exposure was minimal and short, we both reeked, perhaps on a par with the worst run-over skunk highway smell you can recall.

Inside the house the drama accelerated. We watched from the driveway through a big picture window. It was like being at an aquarium watching divers trying to catch a run-amok squid.

Father removed himself to the bar for another scotch, seemingly oblivious to the stench. My stepmother stripped off her dress and threw it to my wife, then took off after the dog. (Avert your eyes, Ian. Hold your nose. Deep breaths.) She finally caught him and rushed out of view toward the front part of the house.

My wife joined us in the driveway, furious that her brand-new dress was ruined. More deep breaths. Father drank his Scotch and turned on the TV. We assumed, of course, that the Homestead trip was a goner, and our next step would be a run to the store for tomato juice, the only product in the world that can cancel skunk odor.

Wrong. After fifteen minutes or so Stepmother reappeared, put on her dress, and she and Father emerged ready to go. The dog, she explained, was given a bath which—lacking tomato juice—hadn't really done much good. So she put him in her bed to soothe his jangled nerves, and closed the bedroom door to keep him from stinking up the whole house. Rather like locking up Mrs. O'Leary's cow after the fire, it seemed to us.

We protested. We couldn't possibly go to the Homestead smelling like road kill. But they would have none of it. We had a reservation, and we were going. We argued the point but in the end relented, though later on we wondered why in the world we gave in.

It was a very long twenty-minute ride. I sat in the back with my head out one window; Ian did the same on the other side. Susan sat in the middle holding her nose and wiping tears out of her eyes. Father and Stepmother chatted casually in the front saying they would have to remember to stop for some tomato juice on the way home if the store was still open. I couldn't imagine how this would play out at the hotel, but one thing was certain: unlike Mr. Ellis, we wouldn't get past the lobby.

When we pulled up to the front door, the Doorman opened Father's door, and instantly reeled back. Father got out and told him not to park it far away. "Far away?" I thought? It'll be right where we left it. But not to worry: they'll toss us out in under three minutes and we can be on our way. I wonder if I'll ever be able to show my face in the place again?

Of all the images left from that bizarre night, the lobby scene is the most vivid. The Homestead lobby is an enormous elongated room 21½ feet high, 175 feet long and 25 feet wide. The front door is at one end, and to get to the hallway leading to the dining room one must walk the entire distance to the other end past the fireplaces, cozy seating areas, and the chamber quartet. It was busy that Saturday night and the lobby was filled with people dressed to the nines, chatting merrily, enjoying the comfortable opulence of one of the Nation's grandest old hotels.

We had barely gotten in the door when the "Dear Gods!" started. At first no one seemed to know where the stench was coming from, but it quickly became clear that we were the cause.

I recall thinking that I finally knew what Moses must have felt at the Red Sea. The parting of the waves preceded us by fifteen or twenty feet—such was our combined skunk power. People fell entirely silent or murmured to each other. Handkerchiefs and tissues were everywhere. But onward we marched, Father at the lead, fastened on getting to the table and a glass of scotch.

The Maitre d'hotel was amazingly cool about it all, and lead us straight away to a table in a far corner almost behind the orchestra. People sitting at adjacent tables were moved.

"Where the hell is my scotch?" demanded Father. It appeared quickly. People stared. It was too much for poor Ian. He fled to the men's room, and tried in vain to wash off the smell. Feeling he might be ill, he stuffed wads of toilet paper up his nose to kill the smell.

Back at the table, Father was halfway through his first scotch and feeling more relaxed. The moment Ian sat down, Father turned to him and asked "So, Ian, now that you're a college graduate, what's the next step? Where do you go from here?"

Poor Ian. Sounding like someone fresh out of nasal surgery and still feeling the effects of ether, Ian tried his best to explain his dilemma about graduate school versus job.

Stepmother was feeling neglected, and asked me to dance. I flatly refused so she turned to Ian. "You can't have the graduate all to yourself," she said to Father, grabbing Ian by the wrist. "He wants to dance with me!"

And so it went all the way through dinner. The waiters made as few visits as they could get away with, obviously doing everything in their power to get us out as fast as humanly possible. Fortunately, there were fewer people in the lobby for the return run, but the effect was just the same. The stench had hardly diminished.

The car—as expected—was almost exactly where we left it. On the way home Ian and I again hung out the windows. Father commented he thought the food was rather indifferent, and the service certainly seemed a bit off.

"The Homestead just isn't what it used to be," he said sadly.

Chapter XIV

Endings

A few months ago I was standing with Granny Cleek's son, June, on the hill at the very end of the hollow overlooking their home place. He was 86 at the time, and still working every day on the farm. I told June I recalled Granny saying her husband had been hit on the head by a falling branch from a tree he was cutting down, and that it led to his death.

"Yes, indeed. I was with him. It happened right over there," he said pointing to the edge of the field. "He was chopping down a chestnut tree and a big 'ol branch fell on him. I was never so scared. He weren't right after that. Died less'n two years later."

He pointed out the trail over the mountain his sister Dorothy hiked to get to the school bus, his slight nod and the look on his face still full of wonder over her persistence. He pointed in the opposite direction to the higher mountain over which his father and grandfather traveled to take their livestock to market fifty miles away. Again, it was said with a sense of wonder and pride in their ability and determination.

We stood on that hill quite a while. I was touched by the simple eloquence of June's recollections, and the obvious reverence he had for the memories of his family's values and accomplishments. His only regret was that the small farms and old home places passed down through generations were being gobbled up by what he termed "city people" who had no sense of the past, and no reverence for the simple beauty of the land.

But in a curiously prophetic way he ended our talk saying he wouldn't have to worry about it. He was going to keep on farming the place until he died.

"After that, I won't have to see it," he said.

A few weeks later June was dead. He had been trimming weeds in the yard and said his back was hurtin' a bit. He climbed into his truck, slumped over, and was gone.

I stood in line at the funeral home, June's open coffin in the front of the room, the family greeting friends in sad resignation. From a distance I couldn't tell it was June, but as we moved slowly closer I saw his hands. His unsmiling face didn't match the June I knew, but the hands did.

June had the hands of a quarterback: immense, powerful spans with angular fingers any one of which seemed twice the thickness of my thumb. Folded on top of each other they dominated the picture. You could take away the man's life and flatten his smile, but the hands that split wood, worked the fields, and wrestled livestock for over eighty years were still strong—and alive.

June's death was hard on everyone who knew him. His honesty and frank humor, his love of traditional music, his faith, and stubborn (but successful) adherence to the "old timey" way of doing things were widely admired, even envied.

His loss was toughest on Whimpy, his nephew and daily working companion. Three months later Whimpy died in his sleep. He was only 67 and seemed in fine health. Everyone was, of course, shocked by his sudden death, but there was general agreement about what caused it: he simply couldn't recover from June's passing. That made perfect sense to everyone who knew June and Whimpy.

Mickey Williams, Frank Williams' wife, is now in her nineties, fragile and petite, and though vascular trouble has ravaged her memory, she remains by constitution and reflex the cheerful, upbeat, uncomplaining person she has been all her life. Even though she doesn't know who her visitors are, she greets each one with her signature smile and enthusiasm. "Golly! It's good to see you. Come on in."

If I close my eyes and forget for an instant what year it is, I can go back fifty years, hear those same words, smell the fresh-baked bread, and know that for a few minutes I will again be one of the Williams boys.

Gene Folks is in his eighties and has come back to Bath to bury his wife's ashes, and to "be a little closer to home, and do some fishin'."

My father died of cancer three years after the skunk episode. At first there was some hope that timely surgery might arrest the process, but in the fall of 1995 it became clear he only had a few months to live. He always spent the winter in Florida, and as the house in Bath was closed up and he prepared to head south for the last time, we all had the feeling he would not be back in the spring.

"You don't know what I'd give to be able to see the Redbud bloom just one more time," he said just before he left. It was said in a matter-of-fact way, ever the engineer sizing up a situation and making an offer. I choked over the remark, but he simply returned to packing. I had hoped that as he neared the end of his life we could talk about the issues that divided us, maybe actually resolve some of our differences, and part in a loving or at least mutually accepting way.

But it didn't happen. He was, if anything, angrier than ever, busy trying to create legal documents to control our destinies from beyond the grave. About a month before he died I tried again.

"Tell me, Father, looking back and seeing what's coming, can you say how you feel?"

"Sure," he said without hesitating, "I've had a perfect life. Nothing ever went wrong. I have no regrets about leaving." End of conversation. A month later I spoke to him by phone, just after he had been hospitalized with kidney failure. He was in a great deal of pain, but what had his attention was his irritation over being admitted by a Chinese on-call physician.

I said I would catch the first plane to Florida and see him in a few hours. As I said good bye and was about to hang up, he said:

"There's something I want to tell you."

"Yes, Dad, what is it?"

"I'll say one thing for dehydration: it does wonders for your arthritis." Then he hung up. An hour later he was dead.

He just couldn't do it. And I can't accept those last words on any level other than admiring his sang-froid in the face of death. But my last recollection of him, the one I often think about, is not that image, or the "perfect life" speech, followed by his statement that firing people was his favorite thing to do, it's a scene I doubt he realized anyone saw. But Gene Fry, our farm manager and close family friend, did see it, and described it for me.

After closing the house, Father and my stepmother stayed at the Homestead for several days before pushing off for Florida. It was near Christmas, and a number of family members joined them for a difficult celebration at the hotel. On the second morning, Father was up for an early breakfast, then without a word to anyone, he and his dog, Ruff, simply disappeared. No one saw him leave or had any idea where he had gone. Still, it wasn't out of character, and there was only slight apprehension over what he might be up to.

Gene stopped by the empty house to check the heat. He saw Father's car parked next to the back door, went in, and through two other doorways saw him sitting in a rocking chair on the porch with Ruff on his lap. Gene silently withdrew.

Rocking gently he stared out across the garden and fields to the barns in the distance. To one side, he could see the old orchard where a log barn stood when he was a kid, a safe place to play well out of his mother's range. On the other side, below the surrounding hills, he could see his parents' house and the lawn where he sent Nootsie, the donkey, to wreck the Madam's garden party. Below the lawn was the pond where he threw the huge brass starter cannon immediately after it blew off his brother Malcolm's right index finger when Malcolm was sixteen. It was the same pond the Madam's car rolled into when she forgot to set the brake. He could see the little dairy where the milk was pasteurized, and butter made and put in boxes marked "Meadow Lane Farm." He could see his backhoe in the machine shed and hear the peacocks scream HELP! HELP!, and watch the flock of guinea fowl dart back and forth looking for bugs the frost had spared. Next to the machine shed, in the middle of his view, was the huge horse barn he had meticulously restored, the center of activity when he was growing up, the place where all the hunts and long rides started and ended.

Later, in the afternoon, Gene came back, but Father was still sitting in the rocker stroking Ruff's neck. Again, he quietly retreated. Father showed up at the Homestead about 5:30 that evening. Asked where he had been, he shrugged and said he had gone for a drive.

After he died, I was put in charge of making a suitable container to hold his ashes. My instructions were to make it big enough for both his and my stepmother's ashes to fit comfortably side by side. There was to be no repeat of the disaster of my grandparents' last burial.

My carpentry skills are only modest, but with some fine old wood, a few tools, and plenty of time between his death and burial (two months, in fact, no need to rush these things), I managed to make something that looked like a cross between a Dexter shoe box and the Parthenon. I put a small South of the Border bumper sticker on the plastic cube of ashes, and sealed the box.

Like his father, mine wanted to be buried on the farm, but not in a forgotten tangle of underbrush on the side of the mountain. Father's Final Resting Place is in a walnut grove next to the old slave cabin where he has an unobstructed five-mile view of the valley.

At the foot of the last hollow in the distance, visible as a tiny speck, is Granny Cleek's farm.

Before Father was installed in his FRP, we quarried a large headstone, and set it in place. Then came the question of what to put on the brass plaque. His wife felt there should be something beyond his name and dates, a phrase to sum up his life, his philosophy or perhaps how we should all remember him.

None of the offerings seemed quite right to her. Especially mine. I came up with several ideas others liked, but she shot them all down.

Then I hit on the solution. "How about 'His Sprit Is In The Land'?" and quickly—before she could say NO!—I added with considerable reverence "It's from Thoreau, you know."

Thoreau? Of course, perfect. And so it is.

One of Father's proudest accomplishments was to put our land into an open air easement, a state-sanctioned device that prevents hacking up farmland for future development. He persuaded other landowners in the valley to do the same, including the family that had arranged to take over the Cleek farm when June eventually died. By this set of contiguous easements, the valley's land and rivers are protected, and his view will be forever unblemished. His spirit may be in the land, but his hand will always be on it.

Father had the resources and steely determination to control his life from both sides of the grave. But for others, it isn't so simple or clear. "What's going to happen to us?"

In one form or another, I heard that sad, haunting question many times while putting this project together. Invariably, it came from older folks watching their way of life disappear, swept away by changes rapidly overtaking the entire region. The Homestead is opening huge areas to upscale residential development. Farming as a way of life has all but disappeared in Bath, and is starting to fade in adjacent areas. A ski resort and mountain development has made remote Pocahontas County, West Virginia, a popular tourist destination. People driving to the slopes unknowingly zoom by Minnehaha Springs, once a spa on par with The Warm and The Hot, and right past the hollow where June Buzzard lived. Little general stores are being replaced by Mini Marts peddling rubber pizza and lottery tickets, livestock markets are shutting down, and Webb's store has become a supermarket.

Father bought the grist mill and turned it into an upscale restaurant with adjacent shops and a small inn. The old water wheel stopped turning a few years back. The mill race silted in and no one seems interested in cleaning it out.

It would be unfair to Father to imply that he simply brushed aside the historical significance of the old grist mill. In spite of the change from historical relic to commercial enterprise, he did largely preserve the mill building. And there is no denying the positive impact the project has had on the local economy.

There is another historical detail worth mentioning, one I doubt a handful of people know. One of the first obstacles he faced in the renovation was the need to remove the enormous 19th-century motor that ran the mill when water power was no longer enough to turn all of the grinding equipment. Instead of simply ripping it out, he researched it and found it to be one of only a few remaining working engines of its sort. At considerable expense, it was carefully removed and sent to a museum in Delaware.

While far from the hollows of Bath, the Hooper's Straight lighthouse, now part of the Maritime Museum in St. Michael's, Maryland, is another of his projects worth mentioning. When he heard the old lighthouse was about to be demolished, he got together a group of conservationists and raised money to have it removed from its foundation in the Chesapeake Bay, transported to St. Michaels, restored and opened to the public. However fixed he was on his own sense of how things should be, there is no denying Father's fascination with history.

His focus, however, was more on grand displays than on the people who grew the crops and operated the old mill. He was interested in great historical figures and significant places, but was aloof from the personal histories of area farmers and merchants. Had he been asked "What's going to happen to us?" I think he would have dismissed it as a whining, concocted message, not a serious question. He never knew adversity, nor was he ever dependent on anyone else to meet his basic needs.

But most of the people I have talked to remember life when times were tough but dependable, and there was a real sense of community. They went to church with their neighbors, helped each other through the Great Depression, and probably knew someone who fought in the Civil War or was born in slavery. These are the last of fourth- and fifth-generation families now reduced to living on a tiny fraction of the farms their great-grandparents worked.

Looking through cracked and faded family albums, they remember their childhood, the old folks, and the lives they all led. They tell you with some sadness that their grandchildren don't have much patience with stories about how they carried water from a well, ate squirrel for dinner, or had to dig snow away from the outhouse to get the door open.

But what is happening in this remote part of rural Virginia isn't unique; no rural place is safe. Old barns are being replaced with tin garages, and pseudo-colonial monstrosities surrounded by plastic fence show up in sheep fields everywhere. Even traditions are subject to the voracious hunger of commercialism.

The Hatfields and McCoys now have a festival, sell coffee mugs and T-shirts, and realtors are selling off the land one lot at a time. It's good for the local economy and, some argue, sort of preserves a little piece of border history.

Elsewhere in Appalachia you can ride through a coal mine in an electric mule, hear about the days when martial law was declared in the coal fields, and Billy Mitchell had planes loaded up ready to bomb rebellious miners.

And you can pause for a latte at the gift shop, or stop by Walmart on the way out of town.

All of this bothers me as it does many with a strong reverence for the past. But next to the anguish of folks watching their entire way of life disappear, my own sense of loss is trivial—even petty. After all, I am both a newcomer and a son of the crowd that started pushing aside the stable mountain culture to make way for its golf courses and tennis courts. As much as I genuinely care about the changes that upset, confuse and often downright anger the bedrock citizens of the area, I have to accept the fact I will always be something of an outsider.

Still, I want to make a statement—several, really—about our heritage, divided as it is. On a personal level I want to do my part to encourage preservation of our past, here and throughout Appalachia. I want people to slow down and wonder what went on when the old buildings at Minnehaha were new and filled with visitors taking the waters, and remember the pioneers not as caricatures on a coffee mug, but as brave, resourceful and determined people.

In spite of significant progress and the outward appearance of resolution, racism persists and cannot be forgotten. Its memory and hurt linger, especially for those who experienced it directly.

My generation is painfully aware of the part some in our family played in the shameful exploitation of African Americans in the past. True, they were equal opportunity exploiters, happy to take advantage of anyone whose status or economic circumstances created vulnerability. But there was a clear difference when it came to racial discrimination, an added quotient of degradation reserved for blacks. It just wasn't enough to take advantage of the person or situation. They had to add a label, epithet or gesture just to make sure the point was made: you're a second class citizen, and don't forget it.

When I started this brief romp through some of my recollections, I had a clear sense of how important and formative they were for me. I felt it would be fun—maybe a bit cathartic—to revisit the places and people who shared or remember some of these events with the same fondness I have. What has surprised and delighted me, though, is the enthusiasm others have for these and other similar tales.

We all agreed that while losing something precious is painful, and while sharing and reliving it doesn't slow the loss, it does reaffirm our extreme good fortune in having known the land and the people of our little part of the world.

Reverence for the past motivates us to preserve the best of what we have for the future. The more we know about the conflicts and struggles of our ancestors, recent and remote, the more we know about ourselves. And maybe that will make us more concerned about how we treat our beautiful land—and each other.

Chapter XV

Acknowledgements

Given the tone of what I have written, my gratitude to everyone who helped with this project should be quite clear, and thanking each and every one would be a tiresome exercise in redundancy. It would be wrong, however, to assume my thanks are limited simply to the telling of stories and use of photographs. Less tangible and not intentionally given, it is the gift of trust and the sharing of deeply personal feelings for which I am most grateful.

When we finished with photo albums and the stories I was tracking, quite often the real memories began, and with them, a great deal of emotion. I think of a visit I had with Dizzy Dean and his wife, Dorothy. I sat down at the kitchen table, got out my notebook, and when I looked up Dorothy handed me a ham biscuit just like Granny Cleek used to do. Dizzy went off to hunt morels with a friend, and Dorothy and I just talked. She reminisced about her childhood, the Depression and her life with Dizzy. Some of it was funny, like how she and Dizzy spent their wedding night in an empty house on Fort Dinwiddie. The house was an old brick mansion built in 1805 next to what little was left of the fort at the time. My grandparents treasured the place and had elaborate plans to restore it and live there. They would not have been happy to think anyone—especially unauthorized honeymooning "locals"—was in their treasured house.

"We didn't have anywhere else to go, no one was there, so that's where we went." I told her what I thought my grandparents' reaction might have been had they found out.

"I know," she said with a wink, and we both howled with laughter.

She could have stopped there, but she went on. Painful as it obviously was, and without any prodding from me, she told me about the aftermath of the shooting, and of the struggle she and Dizzy had both in the family and community. In perspective, it makes any trauma I ever coped with seem pretty small.

That is what I experienced over and over: being welcomed into people's memories, trusted with their vulnerabilities, and awed by their personal and family strengths. I don't have the objectivity to know how well I have been able to describe these feelings and insights, but I know that on an entirely personal, basically selfish level, it is humbling.

There are many others who must be thanked, too. In spite of the writer's adage that stories should tell themselves, in the real world that doesn't happen without a tremendous amount of support.

Most of my Appalachian research was done through the Appalachian State University library; specifically, the W. L. Eury Appalachian Collection. Bath County research was done at the Bath County Historical Society library. I am grateful to Ms. Margo Oxendine, the Society's archivist and General Secretary, who in spite of my occasional jab at the social nature of historical societies, still welcomes me back. Mr. John Hoover, the Homestead Historian, gave me a wealth of information about the hotel, provided an enormous bibliography about area history, and wisely cautioned me which of our local writers was least likely to be historically accurate.

Alice Fortune's granddaughter, Ms. Perlista Henry, provided me with photographs, stories about her family, and a wealth of information about regional black history. She also introduced me to the writings of Margaret Burroughs, and connected me to many members of the black community, making sure—like John Hoover—I met the most accurate sources.

Mr. Roger Anderson, a former Homestead employee, musician and professional photographer, let me review his entire collection of photographs, thousands in all. Mr. Anderson's strong sense of ethics translated into making sure that the Homestead photographs he let me use are all his own, not protected by a Homestead copyright.

I am grateful to writer Stephen Wilson, and editors Ellen Andrews and Kip Requardt, friends who read drafts and gave honest criticism, certainly one of the riskier and more taxing requests one can make of a friend.

Susan Compton, Betsy Wiggers and Linda Morrison deserve gold medals for patience, and persistence with the initial manuscript. Jeremy Leadbetter worked magic with the old photographs.

Finally, thanks to my wife, Susan, for tolerating my absorption in this project and occasional testiness about her suggestions. She has an eye for detail, especially in the mechanics of syntax. That part was easy. But where we sometimes clashed was over her questioning my interpretation and presentation of stories. Was I telling them exactly as they were told? Or was I telling them the way I wanted them told? It's a line easily traversed, and while I didn't always like being challenged, in truth she was sometimes (not that often) right. She has the objectivity I often lack, and almost inevitably my writing improves when I listen.

That shouldn't be surprising: all of us do better when we listen, especially when history is speaking.

End Notes

Chapter 1

1. "Appalachia" is a geo-cultural word officially defined by The Appalachian Regional Commission in 1985 as 195,00 square miles of 13 states from southern New York to Mississippi. Its nucleus includes east Kentucky, western North Carolina, eastern Tennessee, West Virginia, southwest Virginia, and parts of western Pennsylvania. Bath and its northern neighbor Highland County both form part of the eastern boundary of the core of Appalachia.

2. From *The Bicentennial History of Bath County, Virginia; Bacova—the Village*, by Elizabeth McClung; Heritage House, 1991.

Chapter 2

3. In 1901 the Baltimore team moved to New York and became the New York Highlanders. Their stadium was at 168th Street, one of the highest elevations in the city—thus the name "Highlanders." They became the New York Yankees in 1913.

4. Words and music by Louis Lambert, 1863, dedicated to "The Army and Navy of the Union."

5. *A History of Appalachia*, Richard Drake; University Press of Kentucky, 2001.

6. *Appalachian Speech*, Walt Wolfam & Donna Christian; Center for Applied Linguistics, 1976.

7. *Mountain Speech*, Cratis Williams (paper from Mountain Life and Work, undated).

8. *Mountain Range*, Robert Henderson; Facts of File; N.Y., 1997.

9. A word that dates only from 1904; Henderson.

Chapter 3

10. There were two African American communities in the county: Shakerag and Switchback. At least in our house, Switchback was also known as "Potlicker." Historically, racism was not particularly strong in most of Appalachia because people were poor and tended farms, not plantations, so slavery was close to non-existent. Bath County was the exception. It is just east of the Fall line, and slavery did exist there. In 1850 there were almost 1,000 slaves in the county. After emancipation, the white citizens made sure the freed blacks stayed where they belonged, and named their tiny enclaves accordingly. Shakerag has only recently become West Warm Springs.

Chapter 4

11. Slightly abridged—with apologies—from *What Shall I Tell My Children Who Are Black?* By Margaret Taylor Burroughs. Born in 1917, she is an educator, poet, writer, artist, and among her many other accomplishments, founder of the DuSable Museum of African-American History in Chicago. Used with permission from the author.

12. The 24th Amendment eliminated the poll tax in 1964, and the 1965 Voting Rights Act outlawed literacy tests. The 26th Amendment changed the voting age to 18 in 1971.

Chapter 5

13. The Homestead has always been known for its fabulous golf courses. The first tee enjoys its own history: it is the oldest continually used tee in the country.

Chapter 8

14. Recently, at a wedding, I met a young woman who is a counselor at Camp Calumet. She was both dubious and horrified when I told her my experiences. It's not that way now, she said. The camp has flipped 180 degrees. Every camper is precious and competition is outlawed. "We don't have any losers. Everyone wins," she explained. I'm not sure which system is worse, but in spite of the trauma, I think I learned more about the real world than kids playing Circle of Friends. She didn't agree, and seemed to avoid me the rest of the evening.

Chapter 9

15. In the old days virtually everyone made their own soap. Cooking grease was saved in a large drum, then water and Red Seal Lye were added, the mixture was boiled, cooled, and then cut into bars. Before cans of Red Seal were available, wood ash was leached to produce lye. Ashes from the stove were saved and stuffed into a propped-up hollow log. Water was poured in one end, and a bucket at the other end collected the highly alkaline "lye."

16. During the Depression, traps made from discarded wooden boxes were popular throughout Appalachia. With a saw, a few nails, and a small scrap of rubber, a highly effective trap could be fashioned. They were called "Hoover traps."

17. When cornered, groundhogs will often make a whistle-like sound. They are also adept at climbing, and will go up a tree if caught away from their den.

Chapter 10

18. A J. W. Hinkle .50 caliber rifle, serial number 1534. Don't
    bother to ask. It's not for sale at any price.

Chapter 13

19. Spa is a Belgian town in the Ardennes famous for its mineral
    springs. In relatively modern times the word has come to mean
    any therapeutic spring. Early travelers would not have used
    the term. Currently, it has been debased to mean any beauty
    parlor that offers foot massage with pedicure.

20. *The Homestead and Warm Springs Valley*; Stan Cohen; Pictorial
    Histories Publishing; Charleston, WV; 1995.

21. His first visit was on September 25, 1755, two months after
    Braddock's defeat at Duquesne. His second visit was on
    October 18, 1756.

About the Author

Philip Hirsh was
educated at Phillips
Academy Andover,
Yale University and
Jefferson Medical
College. Now
retired, he lives with his wife in Lexington, Virginia—
near the area where he collected his Appalachian
stories. Several of these tales were presented as essays
on NPR radio, and because they were well received,
Hirsh decided to expand them into this book.

Breinigsville, PA USA
21 January 2010
231118BV00002B/4/P